Deadlines a

by
John Jenkins

First published by John Jenkins in 2019.

Copyright © 2019 by John Jenkins
All rights reserved. Published by Jay Jay Enterprises

ISBN 978-1-9164648-1-0

Printed in Great Britain by Book Printing UK

Contents

Contents

Illustrations

v

Dedication

To my wonderful family who provided rocket fuel for my ambition.

Acknowledgements

I can include many of the people listed in the index as friends who have influenced me in the writing of this biography. I have enjoyed their company and their advice and learned from them a great deal about life. When it came to writing this book I must record the professional advice given freely by Norman Giller, (himself the author of more than 100 titles) John Kemp, Paul Thomas and Bert Morgan who all read the ms at various stages. Having worked with them long ago I knew I could trust their expertise and judgement. Any mistakes of fact and skewed opinions which remain are mine. Additional proof reading by Sue was a bonus as was the production expertise of my friend Steve Hughes.

Many people who appear in this book are no longer with us but their friendship has left indelible memories: Ted Dickinson, Max Hodnett, Jim Ashford and Bill Lowe. And I should include their loyal partners and families.

Then there is my inspirational family headed with honour by my late wife June – how I miss her – and our children, their partners and grandchildren. In what truly matters I have been the most fortunate of men. Also worth recognition and thanks have been dozens of people who have worked with me and helped to ensure my success as a publisher. Certainly Anthea Ware and

Mary Hogarth were heroes whose loyalty and support particularly in bad times gave me courage to go on, not to mention my cousin Janet.

There are many, many more who deserve my gratitude and praise. I remember all of you fondly and raise a glass to the pleasures we shared.

Verwood 2019

Prologue

When the announcement came that the *News of the World* was to close, later to be cynically re-launched as the *Sunday Sun* I was not surprised. The revelations concerning phone hacking into private telephone conversations were too serious to be ignored.

For the first time in a lifetime connected with the media I felt ashamed to admit that I was a journalist. I have been a reporter, an editor, with experience on tabloid and broadsheet newspapers; a contributor to some 300 publications and publisher of several magazines and books.

Rebekah Brooks – or Rebekah Wade as she was when editor of the *News of the World* - said that she didn't know that phone hacking was happening. I found that unconvincing.

The *News of the World* was a weekly paper, it came out once every seven days: plenty of time for an editor to find out who is providing stories and where they came from. If she truly didn't know, then she must have been one of the most naïve national newspaper editors of all time.

I once worked for the *Sunday Express* under the editor John Junor when it sold more than 4 million copies each week. Junor read every line that went into that paper whether it was written by a staff reporter, a provincial correspondent, an international news agency or a specially commissioned politician. Nothing escaped his eye whether it was news, sport, features or a diary paragraph.

He read raw copy, page proofs and the printed paper. Woe betide anybody who got something wrong or stepped beyond the bounds of decent behaviour. Dismissal was a fact of life. He was not universally popular among his staff. But popularity is not a requisite for a good editor. When he gave an instruction it was not a subject for debate. But his judgment of events and people was legendary.

My first editor, on the *Dorset County Chronicle* in its heyday, was Heber Bruce, a Quaker and a man of integrity. I was once offered money to keep a court case out of the paper. When I told him, he took my copy and elevated it from a two paragraph filler to an inside page lead.

The tragedy of the *News of the World* affair is not that they exposed people like randy footballers and actors – or cheating and lying politicians – but that they stepped into the blameless lives of ordinary people, some beset by grief.

At a stroke they undid much of the good that newspapers do to preserve our democracy. Much worse, it gave politicians a stick to beat the Press and to step even closer to laws of privacy – including the infamous Non Disclosure Agreements that hide many wrongdoings.

To have watched John Prescott, Max Clifford and Hugh Grant on screen, posing as white knights denouncing newspapers and claiming to be arbiters of good taste stuck in the craw. What a trio.

And Fords, Virgin and other companies set a dangerous example in withdrawing their advertising. Did this mean that in future newspapers were to be subjected to censorship by advertisers?

There was also an attempt to paint Rupert Murdoch as some kind of ogre who led innocent politicians astray. Labour politicians were quick to say he had Cameron in his pocket. Press Lords have always courted politicians just as politicians have courted them. He was good old Roop to left-wingers when the *Sun* supported Tony Blair and the Labour Party, having been weaned away from Margaret Thatcher. When his newspapers switched allegiance he became a devil with horns.

It's often forgotten that while Murdoch's News International published the *News of the World* and the *Sun*, he also publishes the *Times* and the *Sunday Times*.

The fact that the two sober papers sell around 1.5million copies while the *Sun* vies for premier position on weekdays and Sundays, says more about Britain than it does about Murdoch.

It also did not come as a surprise to me to learn that policemen had been paid by the *News of the World*. In my days as a reporter and editor in London's East End I knew that some officers were given 'a drink' by agencies and national newspapers – in the jargon of the time that translated into anything from £25 to £1,000 or a holiday with some excellent shooting.

As far as I was concerned, the offer came the other way. A Detective Inspector in West Ham offered me money for information that might help his team to feel a few collars. We settled amicably for an arrangement that meant that he gave me useful background while I tipped him off about anything I discovered about crime. It was all done over the odd pint or two in a pub away from his officers and my reporters. Neither of us ever broke a confidence, or paid the other a penny.

Now you have the ridiculous situation of police spokesmen hogging the cameras at the end of a sensational court case giving their views on the crime. This may be good for their egos and promotion but I would prefer such reporting to be limited to the judge's remarks.

Which will be the next newspaper to close? Unfortunately it could be the *Observer*, which has never been a happy bedfellow of the *Guardian*. It was always a better newspaper than its daily partner: it rang with authority whether on politics, defence, the arts or sport and it had the guts to support the abolition of hanging before most politicians jumped on the bandwagon.

Recently it has been starved of resources as the *Guardian*, which once survived on the fat profits of the *Manchester Evening News*, has found its losses mounting.

It will not be many years before we have one tabloid newspaper, probably the *Sun-Express-Mirror*, and one mid range paper: the *Mail-Telegraph* and possibly the *Times*.

Television, radio and certainly not social media will take the place of the missing titles. The creeping paralysis of Non Disclosure Agreements to hush up bureaucratic blunders continues to defraud the public. I cannot see social media ending that.

Now I offer my story of a roller coaster life. I have been a paperboy, soldier, newspaper reporter, editor, chairman, publisher, teacher and entrepreneur but essentially always wedded to the written word.

From a fractured, if not broken home, I travelled from the Intelligence Corps at the height of the Cold War to leafy Dorset and on to the East End of London. From Britain to Austria and Australia. Coast to coast in the United States. I had a paradoxical love of animals and bullfighting, enjoyed my family, astonishing successes and dismal failures.

I met and interviewed many of the good and the great, the needy and the greedy, the liars and the cheats, spread evenly geographically and socially. I reported on, and edited everything, from politics to show business, sport to crime.

The fuel for this ambition was my family; still the most important aspect of my life. I enjoy my children and grandchildren, good wine, malt whisky, friends, sport, good books and good food. I made and lost a fortune. It has been one hell of a ride.

As for what appears today as fake news and information in social media reports, I despair at the lack of discipline and editorial control. Many of these outlets glory in power without responsibility, a charge once falsely laid at the door of journalism by Stanley Baldwin. They transcend national boundaries and appear accountable to nobody.

Without paid-for independent newspapers the future does not look good.

CHAPTER 1

You're in the army now

Begin at the turning point in your life has been my advice to those who want to write their biography or, even a family history. Easy to say, not so easy to do. Everybody has several turning points and it's difficult to pick out the special one that had the most dramatic effect.

Take the year 1953 when I was summoned at the age of 18 for two years of National Service. Britain was still suffering from the aftermath of the second world war and Attlee's Labour government, beset by international debt and the threat of the Cold War with Russia turning hot, introduced peacetime conscription to maintain the strength of the armed services.

The law was formulated by the National Service Act 1948. From 1st January 1949, healthy males 17 to 21 years old were expected to serve in the armed forces for 18 months, and remain on the reserve for four years.

By the time my turn came the period had risen from 18 months to two years, largely as a result of the Korean

War. I was one among two million young men called to the colours. It's hard to recall now how opinion was divided among civilians, the armed services and Parliament. Half the regular army thought we would be a waste of time while others realised that if we prepared for war that would be the best way to keep the peace. Both views were rudely shattered.

Mums were mostly aghast. The lucky ones had just got their husbands back alive and now saw their sons were going off to join the brutality of the services...as they saw it. Pacifists were incandescent. Dads were different, especially those who had served in the forces.

Many boys resented having their careers disrupted, whether they were part of the tiny three per cent heading for university or were articled to become accountants or lawyers or apprenticed to become plumbers, electricians or builders.

I had left grammar school with little in the way of O levels and had failed to find an opening as a journalist. As second best I thought I would become a lawyer and after one false start joined a legal practice which offered the chance of articles for five years at a fee of £250 to be paid by my father. My salary, if you could call it that, would be £1 a week for the first year. Friends were joining banks and local government for more than double that without paying a premium.

I re-took and passed some required O levels but by now was far from convinced that law in a provincial firm was for me. My legal practice was so old-fashioned that it refused to take on any litigation, the partners fearing it was beneath them.

Out of the blue the *Bournemouth Times* offered me a job as a junior reporter and articles for three years. One snag: I had to organise deferment from National Service for three years. The Ministry of Labour refused my application. The *Bournemouth Times* said they could not keep the offer open.

My mind was made up. I would quit the law, get my National Service over as soon as possible and then take up journalism. I applied for service in the Royal Navy.

I had been in first the army and then the naval cadets at school and spent a few weeks at Portsmouth aboard the battleship HMS Duke of York and visited submarines and the gunnery school at Whale Island. My father had served in the Royal Navy during WWII and counted himself lucky to be alive.

He had been posted to three aircraft carriers in the Mediterranean but two of them had been sunk and the third badly damaged before he finished his embarkation leave. His final posting was to a Fleet Air Arm base in Canada.

The navy seemed keen to have me and after a day of medicals and tests rather like an intense Mensa and general knowledge session I was one of around 20 selected from 900 to join the Royal Navy. Surprise, surprise.

A Chief Petty Officer came into the room where we waited and said we had been selected to go to the Joint School of Services Linguistics in Bodmin, Cornwall to learn Russian. If we did well there we would go on to Cambridge University for intensive training and continue in the Royal Navy which could include a commission.

Wow! That was fine by me. I was ready to ditch thoughts of journalism for life on the ocean waves. We still had ships in those days. The chief read out the names. Mine was not among them. 'What about me chief?' He glanced again at his list. 'Jenkins, sorry you're not fit enough. You have to be A1 to get a commission in the navy and you are only fit for duties in a light temperate climate.'

I was stunned. I had red hair and sunburned very easily...but this was a serious blow. I had gone from joy to anger to despair in a few hours. I began to walk out of the building in Southampton almost in tears when a voice commanded: 'Where are you going, son?'

'I'm going home, the navy doesn't want me.'

'But the army does,' was the reply, ' over there.'

Under duress I signed on for the mandatory two years in the army expecting to join the Royal Armoured Corps and drive a tank around Bovington. When my papers and travel warrant arrived I was ordered to the Royal Army Service Corps in Aldershot. Could there be anything worse? The RASC was cruelly and unfairly known as Run Away Someone's Coming and has since changed its name to the Royal Logistics Corps. Aldershot, like those other army reception centres, Catterick and Bulford were in our young days synonyms for hell. We were chased from arsehole to breakfast time: threatened, harried, bullied, drilled, scorned and made to feel like third-class animals.

Those who had been in the scouts or cadets fared better than most. Those who had been away from home, either to school or summer camps were ok. Others sometimes broke down like babies. Reveille was a really fun time. Our platoon sergeant would come in dressed in full uniform and polished boots around 5.30a.m. and continue shouting until everybody got their feet on the floor. If anybody was still asleep after this racket he would stamp over to their bed and shout: 'If you're not up in 30 seconds soldier, I'll be in there with you!'

We were all hungry but lunch in a vast hall was far removed from mum's cooking. The orderly officer would come around with a sergeant in tow and ask if there were any complaints about the food.

Most of us knew enough to stay schtum. Not so one brave soul who spoke up. 'What's wrong with it?' inquired the officer. For a moment words seem to fail this soldier then he blurted out: 'It's not fit for a dog.'

The officer picked up the plate and put it on the floor and motioned his dog forward. The obedient mutt wolfed down the lot.

The officer turned to the sergeant. 'Charge that man,' he said.

Anyone who has worn uniform will tell you the best place in the world to make friends is the armed services. In the next bed to me was a quiet-spoken cockney lad called Steve. He was pure gold. Our days were filled with parades, endless cleaning of kit, drilling on the square and sessions in a massive gym. In the gym the PTIs (Physical training instructors) wore red and black T-shirts and were kings. We were serfs. Came the day when boxing gloves were produced. Our PTI put on a pair and selected people from the squad to spar with him. Needless to say, if one was lucky enough to land a blow the PTI unleashed a ferocious counter attack. As one victim returned bruised to his place the PTI threw the gloves towards me. I had done enough boxing to look after myself but Steve caught the gloves before I could move. He must have weighed all of seven stone, wet.

The PTI, who was around four stone heavier and four inches taller than Steve, shrugged and waited for him to move in. There was a sudden blur as Steve unleashed a combination of punches I had not seen outside of the professional ring. A piston left hand crashed over a careless guard into the PTI's face, a right to the body saw his hands drop and that was the signal for another flurry of punches to the head which snapped his head back with a crack against the wall bars only for him to receive more punishment to the body. He had not laid a glove

6

on Steve and was bleeding from the nose and a cut over his eye.

Our roar of delight brought the sergeant in charge over. 'That's enough soldier,' he said to Steve and ordered his corporal PTI to go and get cleaned up.

'You boxed before?'

'Yes sarge. I was London Feds champion last year.'

So that was it. Steve had reached the finals of the London Federation of Boys clubs championship at the Albert Hall and won the title for his weight. It must have been the flyweight championship which was the lightest category in those days – 7stone 7lb. I had picked the right guy as a friend.

Apart from the endless bull I found myself taking more tests and finally an interview with a PSO colonel (personnel selection officer). Looking back I think that colonel was one of the shrewdest interviewers I have ever encountered. He sympathised over my disappointment at not getting into the Royal Navy and offered the opinion that as I was in the army it would be wise to make the best of it. Somehow he got me talking about the Bournemouth Municipal Orchestra where Rudolf Schwarz was the conductor. He had been released from Belsen concentration camp before finding fame in Britain. The colonel seemed surprised and interested that I should know this.

He leaned back and said: 'Ever thought of going into Intelligence?'

That was how a few days later, dazed and astonished, I found myself with 27 others heading for the Intelligence Corps depot at Maresfield in Sussex.

Anywhere would have been better than Aldershot and I was starting to learn that God and the army move in mysterious ways. Little did I realise that even the Intelligence Corps retained many of the army's fundamental views and it would not be long before it was my turn to put on the gloves in the ring. And I would make a friend for life.

CHAPTER 2

They call it intelligence

Maresfield was a totally different army experience. Sergeant McKay, often an umpire at Wimbledon would you believe, met us at we arrived at the station. 'Welcome gentlemen,' were his opening words and several of us looked over our shoulders to see if he was talking to us. We climbed aboard a 3-tonner and 15 minutes later were deposited outside the guardroom at Maresfield depot in Sussex to be met by a ferocious Provost Sergeant in full regalia with white webbing and a red sash. He was backed up by Corporal Christie from the Black Watch whose guttural Scottish commands did not include the word gentlemen, but shorter ones limited to four letters.

We 28 squaddies, hereinafter known as Two Squad, were confused. As Tennyson had put it:

Ours not to reason why,
Ours but to do and die.

Many national servicemen – 395 - had already been killed, mainly in Malaya and Korea. Many more had been wounded. Would our destination be to those hotspots, Cyprus or SHAEF HQ in Paris, the British Army of Occupation in Germany or Austria?

Not much time for thinking, for as promised by our instructors, our feet never touched the ground. Four weeks of infantry training, four weeks of Organisation and Administration, and four weeks on counter intelligence. At any point you could be RTUd (returned to unit) if not up to the mark, so we felt like prisoners on parole who dared not step out of line.

Infantry training seemed to consist of endless drill with .303 Lee Enfield rifles, marching up and down again, firing a variety of weapons from Sten guns to Bren guns, the ancient .303 and a .38 revolver. The Nato 280, Walther PPKs and Glocks had not then been invented.

Training was entrusted to the Black Watch giant Christie with weapon handling overseen by Sergeant Robson, a veteran paratrooper from Arnhem.

We made it through that basic month despite an interruption when we were ferried to the banks of the Thames in outer Essex to fight the worst flooding Britain had seen for a century. More than 300 people lost their lives as the East Coast was engulfed.

We were housed in a derelict WWII artillery barracks opposite Canvey Island and worked 16 hours a day building walls with sandbags. Endless tea, and occasional rum kept us going in bitter January weather. Our beds had no mattresses, only bare springs. The windows had frames but little glass.

On a rare afternoon off I was exhausted and caught a bus to the nearest parade of shops. I ordered a cup of tea and a bun in a tiny café and went for a haircut just to sit down in the warm for a few minutes. Neither the bus conductor, the woman in the café nor the barber would take a penny from me. 'Not you, lad. Thanks for what you are doing.' The kindness, courage and thanks from those ordinary people have stayed with me.

O and A was the Organisation and Administration of other armies. So we learned how many field ambulance units there were in a Russian division, how many tanks, how many machine guns, how many men, how many field kitchens. We had comparisons with other armies, including the United States and ours. The theory was that by interrogating a captured medical orderly, cook or a tank gunner you could assess the strength of the forces against you.

As usual throughout history, the British Army prepared its soldiers for the previous war rather than the next one. Our final month included lectures and exercises on counter intelligence and acquisition of intelligence.

For example, we learned the difference between interrogating an arrogant, well-educated Luftwaffe pilot of a Messerschmitt 109 and a member of the PBI (poor bloody infantry) who had been captured after being

11

shelled and shot at for weeks. But the course also included brainwashing techniques used in Korea. All this was known locally as the FS (Field Security) course. Nobody on the course in living memory had got an A grade, around two a year got a B.

Our numbers diminished week by week as various members of the squad were RTUd and in one case chucked out of the army. Of the original 28 only four of us from Aldershot passed. I was one and my great friend Max Hodnett, later a distinguished journalist and editor, was another. We both scraped a C+ which was reckoned good enough. Several others got Cs and C- which were also passes. Five, however, transferred to Signals Intelligence. The rest were returned to unit.

To celebrate one of our rare 36-hour passes Max and I decided to visit London. A coach dropped us in Victoria and we headed off to see the sights. I think we had about £2.50 between us. This was quite remarkable as the army paid us what they thought we were worth - £1.25 a week each.

I had heard there were cheap hotels in Paddington so we headed there to ensure a bed for the night. We then discovered that most of the places rented by the hour. Décor seemed to include red lights in the windows and nobody could quote us for B & B but offered other services. The penny dropped and we moved on. Our meagre resources did stretch to a cubicle each in a Salvation Army hostel near Bird Cage Walk. There was room for a single bed and a wooden chair. The sheets were clean and there was one blanket. That cost five shillings for the night (25d.) Or you could doss down on the floor in a dormitory for a shilling. (12d).

Having settled a base for Saturday night we went back to the Strand and found a Nuffield Centre where servicemen were welcome. These centres were funded by Lord Nuffield who had built a fortune from Morris Motors. Table tennis, darts, a subsidised canteen, snooker and showers were available as well as a record library with booths where you could listen to your favourite 78s.

In the evening we headed for the theatre and wondered whether or not we could afford to see a revue starring comedian Jimmy Edwards at the Adelphi. It looked as if the theatre was sold out but the commissionaire spotted us and said we could stand at the back. A tip of half a crown (25p) meant he was well satisfied.

We returned to the hostel. In the morning you could build your breakfast piece by piece. Fried bread was a penny, an egg 2d, a rasher of bacon 2d and a sausage 3d. A cup of tea was 2d so for around a 5p (12d in old money) the breakfast was great value.

Some strange magnet drew us to Fleet Street which we gazed at in wonder and then to St Paul's where Max said that as it was the Sabbath we should attend morning service, which we two Methodist non conformists did.

On our return to Maresfield we reckoned that we had spent just over £1, had played snooker and darts, seen a West End show, had bed and breakfast and given thanks to the Lord. Not bad value.

Maresfield was full of strange people. Among outstanding sportsmen were Johnny Pretlove who got five blues at Cambridge and was later President of Kent C.C. and Colin Smith who opened the bowling for Lancashire with Brian Statham and was later knighted as a leading British architect. Pretlove also played football for Corinthian Casuals.

I met him in a washroom and we began talking about sport. 'If you play rugger you'd better keep quiet about it, otherwise you'll never get out of this place.' Like many garrison commanders of that generation, our C.O. wanted to field an outstanding rugby XV. I had a few games of cricket, batting at Number 6. We won every match easily and I never had an innings. The only time I was called on to bowl was if we had a beer match when the real contest ended early. We usually declared at around 200 for 3.

Less exalted but quite exotic was the son of a baron who used to send his chauffeur and Rolls-Royce to collect his offspring from the depot gates when on a 48-hour pass. There was also the son of a brigadier who wanted to commit suicide for not following in his father's footsteps with a commission and a quiet spoken pale-faced Scot who never – as far as I remember - undressed fully the whole time he was there. He kept his pyjamas on permanently under his uniform but took his battle dress off to go to bed. An earlier arrival had been James Goldsmith who married Isabel Patiño, heiress to the Rio Tinto Zinc fortune.

I survived several scrapes, one of which saw me receive seven days Confined to Barracks for arriving back eight hours late from a 48-hour pass and a grudge boxing match in the gym. It ended with me in hospital with bruised kidneys after taking a battering for three rounds. My opponent was in the next bed with concussion.

Strangely the seven days didn't do me any harm. I had to report to the guardroom immaculately dressed around 6a.m. for inspection. Then change into fatigues to clean the guardroom, then to the cookhouse for more chores and despite classes deliver coal, peel spuds and appear at various hours showered and properly dressed for inspection.

The only way this could be achieved was if friends in the squad cleaned your brasses and best boots and pressed your uniform so you could shower and change at lightning speed to avoid another charge for being late or 'filthy on parade.'

On the fourth day I arrived at the guardhouse to clean out the grate and light the fire followed by coating the brick floor in red Mansion polish when the Provost sergeant said: 'You needn't bother with that today, make us a brew and have one yourself.'

From that moment on I was on first name terms with the sergeant and his two corporals. Funny place, the army, I thought, and went on embarkation leave before being posted to Austria.

On the day leave ended my girl friend June, later my inspiration and wife, cried as we said goodbye on Bournemouth station. She was a student nurse and the loveliest, most honest and loyal person I have ever met. We were just two among thousands of teenage lovers who had the chance to mature and grow up a little before facing life. Meanwhile I was heading towards the Iron Curtain.

The British army had most of its troops garrisoned in Germany and Austria and a dozen of us travelled across London to Liverpool Street station on the way to a troopship at Harwich. From there we sailed to the Hook of Holland and on various trains to bases in Germany – where I said goodbye to Max – while I travelled on to Klagenfurt in southern Austria. I was to make that trip several times.

We gazed out of steamed-up windows at mountains, rivers, Alpine villages and industrial centres. On the way I played cards with two old sweats who had re-enlisted. My father's advice echoed in my head: 'Just remember that you have to learn to take orders before you give them and no matter how good you think you are [at boxing or cards] there is always somebody who can give you a good hiding.'

16

I spent the first half of the journey losing my money and the rest of the time winning it back as I realised that cards in the army was not like a friendly game at home or school.

At Klagenfurt we were housed in a light and airy Jaeger Kaserne barracks captured by the 8th Army from the Wehrmacht. Plenty of room, good showers and excellent sports facilities. Hitler had looked after his troops better than the British War Office. We were a stone's throw away from the Worthersee, an enchanting lakeside resort where we went swimming and in the evening frequented the Crusader Club, a bar for British other ranks in the town. The Crusader had been the battledress badge for the 8th Army. One of our group, who had never had an alcoholic drink in his life, decided to sample one of everything from the spirits and liqueur list. He nearly died from alcoholic poisoning.

We hung around for a week while persons unknown decided where we would be stationed. Some went to Graz, some stayed in Klagenfurt and my luck held. I was posted to Vienna. It was June 1953. Vienna was in the Russian zone behind the Iron Curtain, a city immortalised in Sir Carol Reed's 1949 film *The Third Man* staring Orson Welles and Joseph Cotton, from a story by my favourite author, Graham Greene. Check it out online. It's a masterpiece.

It captured, as I was soon to learn, everything about that romantic, deadly city in the post-war years. Vienna was divided into four sectors: British, Russian, American and French. It was a hotbed for spies, crooks, black marketeers and a battleground for the intelligence services of the occupying powers. Who had the best intelligence service? None of them. That accolade fell to the Vatican that had a volunteer network of priests throughout Eastern Europe motivated by principle not by money. The head of their service was a chess grand master who lived in a tiny flat in Vienna with a voluptuous blonde. His income derived from setting chess puzzles and writing articles on the game for various European newspapers. His network of intelligent intelligence priests knew more than our contacts inside European governments.

We were housed in a section of Schoenbrunn barracks that had been built for élite SS Officer cadets. Since that day I have stayed in worse three-star hotels.

Half our unit – we called it city detachment - were housed in a spacious old flat in the thirteenth district. Two Austrian cleaners looked after us and were rewarded with soap powder and cigarettes which were better than currency in those days for Austrians.

Other NCOs in the Intelligence Corps worked in Int.Org. (Intelligence Organisation) which was a back up and briefing centre for our own sources behind the Iron Curtain.

Hence our job included low-grade intelligence work, sifting information and interrogating illegal frontier crossers. These were Hungarians, Czechs or Yugoslavs who had escaped from behind the Iron Curtain and wanted life in the west, usually the United States but often Canada or the United Kingdom. To get to us they had to cross minefields and barbed wire. Then they faced guards in watchtowers and fearsome trigger-happy border patrols. Many didn't make it.

We NCOs, mostly sergeants, did the preliminary interrogation and sifted out the best for attention by senior officers.

For years afterwards the army used to send me forms to renew my pledge to the Official Secrets Act. Now, what seemed so important then, is small beer.

I did 18 months in Vienna and enjoyed it immensely. I went to the opera in season, ate in some superb restaurants, learned passable German and a smattering of Russian and grew up. I numbered a British newspaper correspondent, Ritchie McEwan and an Austrian journalist, Pepe Kirschner as contacts and friends. There was also a dashing French sergeant from the Chasseur Alpins, Jean-Paul, who was as mad as a hatter and great fun.

These three added so much to my knowledge of Vienna that they are worth a mention. Ritchie had been in the I Corps with the 8th Army through the desert in North Africa and into Austria where he had been demobbed and married an Austrian girl. He wanted to stay in Vienna and through family contacts had snapped up a job as Vienna correspondent for the Kemsley chain of papers, later bought by Roy Thomson and then by Rupert Murdoch. Without knowing it, Ritchie taught me much about the black art of journalism. He assumed that I would follow him as a foreign correspondent. 'Always have your mail sent care of the embassy and always flirt with the plainest girl there. This gives you an excuse to call in every day and meet the Press attaché on equal terms and you get accepted as part of the furniture.' His boss at Kemsley's foreign news service was Ian Fleming of James Bond fame and the service was called Mercury.

Pepe was the nearest thing to a tabloid journalist in Austria and had been a member of the Hitler Youth. We had endless arguments as he insisted that had I been in Austria pre 1939 I would have joined the Hitler Youth, 'the only organisation which got things done.' Years later I received a letter from him to say he had gone to Switzerland and joined Moral Rearmament. Once a fanatic, always a fanatic, never mind the cause.

The more I think about Vienna the more I realise that this book could be devoted to that alone but it's best to summarise the ups and downs. Jean Paul gave me entrée to the French 108 club in Mariahilferstrasse where the girls were not as mercenary as those who frequented the American forces equivalent: The Tux.

We checked and recorded UK passengers at Schwechat airport who were on their way to the Communist sponsored WFTU (World Federation of

Trade Unions) conferences in Budapest. They were always fellow travellers (members of the British Communist party) and frequently trade union leaders. Nobody else could get a visa to travel through the Iron Curtain.

Through a chance meeting at the Prater (Vienna's famous fairground) in the Soviet sector I bought Zorki cameras from Russian pilots for £15 each. These cameras were superb copies of the famous Leica M3.

The pilots had flown the latest MiG fighters into Hungary and were in Vienna on 48 hours leave. Pilots are pilots in any language and out for a good time. For £15 you could have a memorable weekend. In the end I bought many of these cameras for friends in my unit and a few for the Economic Intelligence Unit based in Lacon House, Holborn in London. The latter were bought with what the army termed Ib funds.

A much more dangerous exercise was interrogating German soldiers released by the Russians after ten years or more in their forced labour camps. This was known as Operation Heimkehrer (homecoming) and began in 1954. The first to be released were those who had lost limbs. Some of these had been taken at the siege of Stalingrad or the huge tank battle of Kursk when the Russians killed and captured huge numbers of German soldiers.

I wonder what kind of fool behind a desk in the War Office thought that having been released after years in captivity and returning to homes now within the Russian Zone of Austria, would dare talk about their experiences to any representatives of British military intelligence? And what use would it be? The released prisoners were still terrified of the Ivans. If you want an example of their experiences read Colonel Hans von Luck's story, *Panzer Commander,* one of the best books on war ever written. Colonel Luck later lectured at Sandhurst.

A welcome bonus was the array of bookshops in Vienna. The British, Americans and Russians all vied with each other to offer brilliant selections at knockdown prices. I bought several volumes of works by Tolstoy, Turgenev and Dostoevsky.

My colleagues in Vienna seemed to embrace people from all backgrounds: public schools, grammar schools, universities, brilliant linguists, cartographers, eccentrics and survivors from WWII German PoW camps.

Some could translate Greek or Latin idioms on the run, others played squash, rugby or football to county standard and others couldn't catch a ball. I ran the cricket team which meant that anybody who could run or catch played. I had one excellent bowler on Leicestershire books who could swing it like Bedser (or Jimmy Anderson if you prefer) and a leg break bowler who stood six feet five inches in his socks and once every four overs could produce a leg break on a matting wicket better than Shane Warne's best. The trouble was that the other 23 balls could disappear for 60 or 70 runs. We made the final of the British Troops Austria only to lose to the Royal Engineers whose skipper plundered 60 in around ten overs.

Ken Marshall, who played rugby for Cornwall, coached me to play as a full back. Hence after soccer in the morning I would often play rugger in the afternoon. Another member of the unit was an outstanding hockey player and persuaded me to play in goal. Hockey in the army seemed like organised mayhem.

After one football game, in which for some reason I played in goal against RAF Schwechat, I was kicked in the head diving at the feet of a player called Gemmell who later turned out for St Mirren. I woke up in hospital surrounded by nuns all wearing huge tri-cornered white hats that looked like lampshades. In those days Gina Lollobrigida and Sophia Loren seemed to play either nuns or loose women in films. For a moment I thought I had gone to heaven. Some disappointments are still heavy on the memory.

Thanks to George Lester, who was on Arsenal's books, I was introduced to Herr Schick, manager of Vienna Rapide, the crack Austrian side. They had been the first side from 'the west,' to play against Spartak and Dynamo in Moscow and he gave me pictures of their matches played under floodlights – an amazing innovation at the time.

This led to my first published magazine article: If Arsenal Go to Moscow in *World Sports* magazine.

Two survivors from WWII who had learnt their German in prison camps were drafted into the Intelligence Corps when the Allies spent most of late 1945 and 1946 hunting Nazis who had gone to ground. Harry York's German had a Polish accent, which told you where he was imprisoned and Fred, whose surname I have forgotten, suffered from Stalagitis. Or as one of our Hungarian translators put it: *Zat Fred, he is, ow you say, round ze bend.* She had it right but he was still a very smart interrogator while Harry had what war correspondent Tom Pocock once described as an essential quality for a journalist: a degree in low cunning.

Unknown to me a young National Serviceman called David Cornwell was doing a similar job to mine in the British zone. He went on to have a long career in intelligence later followed by enormous literary achievement as a novelist. He's much better known as John le Carré. Long before this I had twigged his background because he named one of his civil service characters Lacon, presumably after Lacon House.

Even le Carré couldn't have made up the name of our CO, Major Lionel von d'Hardinge and above him Colonel Dangerfield. I doubt if John Buchan could have got away with it.

In between all this low-grade skulduggery I learned to play squash, hockey, rugby and dealer's choice poker. In addition I learned the hard way how not to drink to excess. I also began to write magazine features that were published and took a turn or two on the local British Forces Network radio station.

My connections to local journalists were seen as a benefit and a danger. I was wrongly accused of tipping off Pepe about the Czech security services plan to kidnap the star of an ice show that was performing in Vienna. They thought she was going to defect to the west and we thwarted their plans to masquerade as carpet fitters, enter the hotel and kidnap her rolled up in a carpet. I had been asked to check with Austrian police to find out where she was staying but I didn't need to as Pepe was dating her and told me she was in a hotel in Hietzing. The following day all the Austrian newspapers carried a front-page story to say British Intelligence had thwarted a plan by the Czechs to kidnap their ice star and take her home.

Not until the manager of the ice show admitted that he released the story to gain publicity for the show was I off the hook. Nevertheless I got a rap over the knuckles for not revealing to my commanding officer that I was writing for British magazines.

Somehow I never thought that my articles on sport, food, wine, travel and fashion were worth bothering him with. But regulations are regulations even in the Intelligence Corps. One of the magazines was *Soldier*. I had done a few broadcasts for BFN whose station manager in Vienna was Major Ferguson. He had been seconded from the Northumberland Fusiliers and was a genuine action man, broadcasting from the bottom of the Danube to the top of the Prater big wheel. He was also something of a Professor Henry Higgins and could point to your place of birth or upbringing with incredible accuracy. He listened to my voice and said, 'could be Hampshire or could be Dorset.' Well, I didn't have the rich tones of John Arlott but he was dead right. I was born and grew up in Bournemouth on the Dorset-Hampshire border.

I still diced with army regulations. Possibly another breach occurred when June spent one of her holidays with me, travelling by ferry and train across Europe into the Russian zone to stay at the Hotel Viktoria in Hietzing. We spent much time together thanks to friends in my unit who covered most of my duties. There was no doubt in my mind: this was the girl I was going to marry – if she would have me. On her last morning I remember sitting on a seat in the Ringstrasse counting our money to see if we had enough to dine again at the Griechenbeisl Restaurant, (a favourite of Schubert and Strauss) in the shadow of Stephanskirche, and still leave enough for her to journey safely home.

Every month there was a parade by the occupying powers when whoever was in the chair handed over control. The French handed over to the British who handed over to the Americans who handed over to the Russians. This was a big propaganda occasion. The Russians flew in the Red Guards and the Red Army choir. The Americans paraded the 2nd Tactical Air Force Band and the French the Chasseur Alpins who seemed to march at the speed of Olympic sprinters. But the real show stoppers for the Viennese, who turned out in their thousands, were the Pipes and Drums of the Camerons.

Another great regiment which manned the Vienna garrison was the Green Howards. They embodied all the virtues of a fine infantry regiment, from the colonel to the most junior subaltern's wife. I felt it a real shame when, in the face of yet more defence cuts, the regiment was merged into the Yorkshire Regiment in 2006.

The Russian's trump card was a visit to Vienna by their WWII hero Marshal Zhukov who masterminded the defence of Leningrad against the Nazis and led the Red Army into Berlin. Imagine the popularity of Eisenhower and Montgomery at the height of their fame and then double it. That was how Russian soldiers greeted Zhukov. Charismatic did not do him justice as a description.

A few years later June and I went to Earls Court in London to see the Red Army choir. Behind us sat old Vienna hands George Lester (who had qualified as an accountant) and Mick Copson who was 'something the Foreign Office.' For an encore the Red Army burst into Treblinka and we all joined in lustily remembering what Russian we could. This was a bitter, ironic song about the German concentration camp in central Poland. Nearby spectators must have thought we were members of the Communist Party of GB!

As my time in Vienna was approaching its end Ritchie McEwan asked if I would like to stay on in Vienna as his leg man. He not only represented Kemsley but also a North American wire service and another chain of newspapers. It was tempting. I had covered a couple of international football matches for him as Ritchie knew nothing and cared less about sport. One match was Austria against the famous Hungarian side under Puskas and the other, Austria against Wales who had Trevor Ford and Derek Tapscott inflaming the local fans with their tactics and tackling. I rather liked the view from the Press Box in the Prater Stadium. This Hungarian side were superb and later beat England 6-3 at Wembley, the first home defeat we had ever suffered there.

After a lot of soul searching I took advice that it would be better to go home and learn journalism from the bottom. The army also suggested that I should sign on as a regular and apply for a commission. However, they would not guarantee that the commission would be in the I Corps so that was a non-starter.

The euphoria of demob was a strange experience. I met up again with Max. He was on his way back to a job on the *Derby Evening Telegraph*. One poor mutt who failed the FS course had spent nearly two years in the blanket store at Maresfield, delighted that he could go home every weekend. Max and I who had been swapping stories about our adventures abroad shook our heads. That was the other side of the National Service coin.

As I sign off from the record of my service for Queen and country I will place on record that the regimental march of the Intelligence Corps was not: *See them Shuffle Along* and that ribald verses to the tune of *Dear Old Sussex By the Sea* do not appear in any military manual.

Deadlines all my Life

CHAPTER 3

My attempt to libel the Lord Chief Justice

At the age of 20 the world is your oyster but mine didn't seem to have many pearls. Despite a book full of magazine cuttings written during the previous two years, a story sold to the *News Chronicle* about Austrian Thalers (gold coins which rivalled sovereigns for currency in the Middle East) and an article on my army experiences for the *Bournemouth Echo* nobody wanted to give me a job as a reporter.

I had several memorable interviews. One with the *Bournemouth Echo.* Things seemed to be going well. The editor, Rodney Andrew, asked me for an article on my National Service experiences that I duly supplied, which made a full page. During the interview a messenger brought in Press Association copy on Stock Exchange prices for the day that he proceeded to edit. I asked him whether the market was up or down and his reply was to ask me if I understood 'these things.' I did because I had

31

worked in my legal days realising funds from the sale of shares for various estates of the deceased rich and leisured in Bournemouth.

'I'm the only one here who understands it,' he said ending the interview with a question to me: 'Why don't you become a stockbroker?' When he didn't offer me a job I sent him a bill for my article and picture for which I received £5 17s 6d.

I also trawled Fleet Street and had a memorable interview with Kenneth Hord, a legendary News Editor of the *Daily Mirror*. I pointed out that I would *prefer a job as a foreign correspondent*. He pointed out that this was the peak of the profession and (I quote) *that I was wasting his fucking time*.

I was not to know then that Fleet Street news editors lived on a diet of raw meat, single malt whisky and draught Bass.

The *News Chronicle* staff were kinder and accepted a brief item. They told me to stay in touch but to consider heading to provincial papers to learn the trade. Still I didn't give up although by now my funds saved from magazine articles were running low and I had signed on, in the words of the day, with the Labour Exchange, where a lady suggested that I might consider a job as an advertising copy writer. No way.

Back to London and a trawl around magazine offices. Surely my book of cuttings would do the trick? It nearly did at Amalgamated Press which had a stable full of popular, low cost titles. The editor of one title had no vacancy but he phoned all his other editors for me while I waited, but nobody had a job.

Two people retained their faith in me: June and my mother.

At last, in response to a battery of letters I was invited to an interview in Bridport, the home of three local newspapers: the *Bridport News,* the *Dorset County Chronicle* and the *Weymouth Times.* I was hired as a junior reporter. It was March 1955 and my pay was £5 a week rising to £7. I had been better off in the army.

I didn't realise at the time how lucky I was. Sam Street was my news editor. He was a French Canadian who had been captured early in the war and imprisoned by the Nazis in Poland. He was like a big grizzly bear and had worked on papers ranging from the *Winnipeg Free Press* and *Chicago Tribune* to the Paris office of the *Daily Mail* and in London the *Daily Express.* An ulcer had forced him into semi-retirement in Dorset. In comparison, Ken Hord was a patsy.

Under Sam's unforgiving tutelage I was soon to learn the basics of the job, covering the Dorchester Assizes, fatstock prices, Southern League football, Minor Counties cricket, the Imperial Services Boxing championships, politics, crime, inquests, the Dorset Music Society and all the humdrum stuff that makes a good local paper.

Even better, with a job I could now ask June to marry me. She was on night duty as a nurse and one Saturday morning we wandered through the pleasure gardens in Bournemouth where the crocuses were just starting to appear and I formally proposed.

I didn't get down on one knee. I hugged her so tight that not only could she not get away (I was not going to give her the chance to escape) she could hardly breathe. She had to nod yes, and that was more than good enough.

We then retraced our steps to Bournemouth Arcade where I spent the last of my savings on an engagement ring.

Life was looking up. Unfortunately parents didn't see it that way. We were too young, too hasty and in the eyes of June's parents I was far from suitable. In their position I would have thought the same. My mother considered June rather stand offish when actually she was painfully shy. Both sets of parents changed their minds in time and offered unstinted support.

My efforts on the Dorset papers were going well and I was given the job of covering the Assizes in Dorchester, which had moved to a new, purpose-built court from the Old Corn Exchange where the Tolpuddle Martyrs had been tried.

To mark the occasion the Lord Chief Justice, Rayner Goddard, presided on the opening clutch of cases. What a calendar he dealt with: murder, manslaughter, carnal

34

knowledge and fratricide. It seemed that every sin was covered.

I worked my socks off getting page lead after page lead. It seemed to go well despite the fact that my shorthand was useless. Goddard was merciless as far as defendants were concerned and brusque to the point of rudeness to junior counsel. His idea of a lenient sentence for somebody who had pleaded guilty to manslaughter, which involved considerable extenuating circumstances, was a 14-year prison term. Even in those days, when hanging was still the punishment for murder, there was a gasp in court at the sentence.

On the way back to the office from the court one day I spotted the Judge Jeffreys' coffee shop in the main street. The famous hanging judge made his reputation at the notorious bloody assizes in Dorchester where, in the Oak Room of the Antelope Hotel, 251 survivors from the Monmouth Rebellion were sentenced to death. It was production line justice. While only 74 of these sentences were carried out, the brutality of the executions ensured they would live long in the memory. As was traditional for those convicted of treason, the condemned men were hung, drawn and quartered, and their heads displayed on spikes in Dorchester and surrounding villages.

What could be better than a succinct diary paragraph, for which we reporters got an extra ten bob, drawing comparisons between Judge Jeffreys and Lord Chief Justice Goddard? A worthy successor.

I used to go to the Press at Bridport at least once a week to see the papers put to bed. The equipment would not have fazed William Caxton who invented the printing press in the 15th century.

The editor of the papers was Mr Heber Bruce, a man of principle and a Quaker. Frequently he would see me hanging about and dictate his leader to me. It was always the last thing to go into the papers. He also took pains to explain what was happening, in the print shop and why, as the ancient flatbed Wharfedale press clattered away.

On this occasion, however, a secretary asked me to go up to his office. I knocked politely and went in. Perhaps I was going to get an increase in pay?

He left me standing and stood with his back half turned away from me gazing out of the window with his hands clasped behind his back. The military call it 'a meeting without coffee.' At last he spoke.

'Jenkins, if you are going to libel somebody I'd rather you didn't choose the Lord Chief Justice.'

Gulp. Thank heavens Quakers believe in justice, truth, pity and mercy: particularly the last two. I kept my job and vowed to study the law regarding defamation. Fortunately he had spiked my diary paragraph.

Events were moving swiftly in other directions and June and I decided to get married sooner rather than later. It would be fair to say that the event was not greeted with joy by either sets of parents but our good friends Don Gardiner, at the time serving in the Royal Air Force, and Barbara Barnes were delighted to be best man and bridesmaid, sharing our joy. The Reverend David Francis of St George's Methodist church in Boscombe conducted the service and as a wedding present gave us back his fee and his blessing. He also tried hard to alleviate the fears of my new in-laws.

We rented a charming, furnished cottage in Sturminster Newton for six months from the author James Stern and his German wife. Included in the deal was the loan of his ancient Austin Seven, his cat and his stool in the bar of the Red Lion next door. Total rent? £3 a week.

Stern used to spend six months in the UK and six months in New York. He wrote wonderful short stories but lived mostly on his ability to translate German fiction and classics into English for American and British publishers, with the help of his wife. 'You won't make any money as a writer,' he once warned me.

Money was a problem. The combined wages of a student nurse and junior reporter allowed for a standard of living comparable to church mice. And the student nurse was pregnant. Today it would be no big deal but the matron at Bournemouth Hospital thought it ranked as a mortal sin.

For those of you who know a bit of Latin that is *peccatum mortale* which can lead to damnation if a person does not repent before death. I think we celebrated.

On the second day of my visit to Dorchester Hospital maternity ward, where Howard was born, I told June that the six-month contract on our cottage was coming to an end and we were going to London because I couldn't earn enough money in Dorset to provide for her and my son and heir. How on earth did she put up with me? I was quitting home and job and moving her to London as she lay nursing her baby two days after his arrival. There's no doubt that these two were my inspiration and guiding light, rocket fuel for my ambition. Although I would have died for them, a decent job with a better salary was a more pragmatic goal.

One important first task was to travel to Stroud in Gloucestershire to show Howard to June's grandparents. Their love for June, who had been in their care during the war years, and her baby, and acceptance of me was heart warming.

I wrote more than 30 letters for jobs and got one on the *Leyton Independent* in East London provided I could find somewhere to live. That was not easy. Leyton, which had suffered during the blitz, had thousands of families on the housing list. I found a rundown apartment above a shoe repairer in Leyton High Street.

We moved up with our total belongings, first in a tiny trailer and a borrowed little Morris. Then by train, with Howard in a carrycot, and a couple of cases.

Two days later I began work as chief reporter of the *Independent.* In desperation I had applied for a job as an ordinary reporter, but after the editor, Dick Harold, had read my cuttings and quizzed me about my National Service he asked if I thought I could do the job as a chief reporter.

I had four other reporters and Harold told me that they were 'a tough bunch of boys.' Two of them, Paul Thomas and Bill Chiles, remained friends for life. In fact it morphed into an excellent little team, playing snooker all Monday afternoon in the Green Man after we had filed the weekend copy in the morning. This meant we had to work 14 hours on Tuesdays and Wednesdays to make up the time but we didn't mind that. Others included Bill 'Stormy' Morris and Ron Newsome.

Our flat today would be condemned. It had a bathroom where an ancient geyser exploded with a roar if you could get it alight and gushed boiling water into a chipped bath. A coal fire in a lounge which boasted an armchair with a busted spring which could cause serious injury if you sat down carelessly, and a dusty staircase up which floated endless leather dust from the shoemaker below working on a lathe. The curtains, threadbare as they were, did not meet in the middle so passengers on London buses trundling down Leyton High Road could look in and wave. That plus the odd rat was home. Not exactly the comforts which June and I had been used to with our parents.

Then I discovered that one of my reporters was being paid £12 a week against my £10. I stormed down to see the editor and got that sorted.

Still, we had little money with the flat costing £4 a week. I learned that my colleagues were adept at selling filler paragraphs and stories to the three London evening papers, the *Evening News* the *Evening Standard* and the *Star*. Fillers were paid at 10/6d which was half a guinea and a couple of cheques for around £20 or so at the end of the month were very welcome. There was fearsome competition from other reporters selling what was known in the trade as lineage.

June weighed in by typing envelopes at home for a mail order company on my portable typewriter. I think she got around £1 for 100 addresses – or was it per 1,000? That typewriter, a Bluebird portable, a gift from my mother on my 20th birthday, has pride of place in my study.

On one side we had the *Walthamstow Guardian* which had a clutch of good reporters including Eddie Vale whose area was Leyton and on the other side we had the *Stratford Express*, Britain's largest selling local paper, with Peter Whaley who earned so much money from lineage that he took a drop in total income when he moved from Stratford to become property correspondent on the *Daily Mail*.

Eddie was later a star reporter for the *Daily Mirror* and he was my fiercest competitor. One night at

Walthamstow Greyhound track, Ken Willson, another local reporter, and I had lost our money and, as was often the case, repaired to Eddie's home where we were in a big card school which included Eddie's mother-in-law. She was known to everybody as Sis. Thank heavens my card playing skills were better than my gambling exploits on dogs.

As a thank you present we decided that Eddie's ma-in-law should have a slap up evening in the restaurant at Walthamstow in return for putting up with us.

There she sat in splendour in the restaurant with her programme while we ensured she had everything she needed. Would she like a bet? Yes, the dog in the black and white striped jacket. Beginner's luck and she won. Next race, which one would she like?

'Oh I think the one in the black and white jacket again.' Another win.

Third race and Eddie asked her: 'I suppose you want to back the six dog again?'

'Oh no, Eddie, I think he must be tired by now,' she said.

People were always joining and leaving and at one farewell party in Walthamstow I met Mike Gabbert. I had first met Mike at the Winter Gardens in Bournemouth when we were covering the Imperial Services boxing championships, Mike for a Hampshire paper and Press Association, me for my local papers and Exchange Telegraph.

He had just been appointed to the *Walthamstow Post*. He, too, remained a friend until ill health brought about his early death. Mike later won the Hannen Swaffer award for investigative journalism when he was responsible for unmasking corruption in football for which several players went to jail. By then he was leading a team for the *Sunday People* and was quickly signed up as associate editor of the *News of the World*, their rivals.

Apart from filling up the *Independent*, which was a huge broadsheet, each week, my other priority was to find a better flat. Still, life had its lighter moments.

Came a knock at the door one night and I traipsed downstairs to find my old army buddy Max clutching a bottle of brandy.

His greeting was typical. 'Bloody hell, Jenkins, you aren't half difficult to find.'

He had used a holiday to trace me through four addresses.

Learning that I was married he asked nervously if June would mind him bringing in a bottle of brandy. 'Not if she gets her share, mate,' and he relaxed.

Then Jim Ashford, a friend from school, who was learning hotel management at the Cumberland, arrived. He had met a South African 'girl of his dreams,' among a crowd of hecklers at Hyde Park Corner and was leaving his job to go to Paris with her. Would we look after his few belongings and after a suitable interval contact his parents to say he was ok? No problem.

Then he asked, 'When did you two last go out together for an evening?' We couldn't remember. 'Off you go, I'll look after Howard.'

We went to the cinema and saw Burt Lancaster and Tony Curtis in *The Sweet Smell of Success.* It was wonderful, just like going out on a new date.

Howard now had two adopted uncles: Max and Jim who thought the world of him.

During a Sunday afternoon stroll with June, and Howard in the pram, we stopped to look at the advertisements in a newsagent's window. There was a two-bedroom flat advertised, the top half of a house, but no mention of who to contact and the shop was shut. It also said that the tenancy was not for people with children.

By shielding our eyes from the sun we made out the address written on the back of the postcard. We shot round to Queens Road in Leytonstone and knocked on the door to find a Mrs Advice. She was the widow of an ex Indian army officer. She was pleasant and mentioned that she had said 'no children.'

'Of course you did,' I said, switching on as much charm, as I could, ' but if the parents are all right usually children are well behaved.'

She peered into the pram. Howard took her finger in his little hand and smiled at her. We were in. The flat was light and airy in a pleasant side street and a couple of steps up from where we were living.

Meanwhile, on the international front, Britain and France decided to invade Egypt and seize the Suez Canal. Eisenhower and John Foster Dulles – with the best of intentions - pulled the plug on that doomed venture. I was two groups away from being recalled to the army. The net result was petrol rationing and the loss of international prestige. That's always the trouble when politicians like Sir Anthony Eden act with what they think are the best intentions.

One Wednesday afternoon, stuck for a lead story, I sent my reporters out to bars and clubs to try to find somebody who had a father or son in the Suez landing. No luck. Then, just before the office downstairs closed a kindly, old lady walked in and said, 'Were you looking for me? My son was wounded at Suez.'

Her son was a paratrooper who was shot as he floated down in the Canal Zone. He had been the first to be evacuated to Cyprus and had written a superb letter to his mother describing the whole landings. She also produced her best picture of him at his passing out parade. The story wrote itself: the first uncensored account of the Suez debacle, under the heading: *Dear Mum, they shot me!*

There were protest meetings about Britain's action in Suez and I covered one where Reg Sorensen, Labour MP for Leyton, whipped up a crowd in a packed Town Hall. He finished with these words: 'I will leave this meeting, walk up the road to the tube station and travel to Westminster to support a vote of censure against this piratical government.'

Sure, he voted as promised. But he didn't go by tube. He had a chauffeur-driven Humber waiting outside. I mentioned that in my report.

Nevertheless, I respected Reg and often met him at the Commons. He was a lay preacher and a genuine asset to the community. He showed me around and got tickets for me to watch a debate which I covered. Labour had Hugh Gaitskell and Jennie Lee (widow of Nye Bevan) lined up against Enoch Powell (later to write for me) introducing prescription charges.

I was with Reg when he was showing a party of American tourists around Westminster. At the end of the tour one lady tried to press five shillings into his hand. 'Madam, please...' he began.

'Whassa matter? Ain't it enough?' she responded.

One story to stick in my mind concerned the funeral of Tommy Smithson, victim of a gangland war. The cortège meandered through the East End towards Manor Park cemetery. The hearse and following vehicles were decked out with floral tributes in what Kenny Everett would correctly call the worst possible taste. Dice and playing cards were chief among the items. The streets were lined with East Enders rather like the turnout for a Royal Wedding or Cup Final victor's parade.

Interspersed in this crowd were plain-clothes coppers, many from the notorious Flying Squad and journalists from every paper. I was one of the latter.

To add to this bizarre scene the hearse got a puncture. Time for a few policemen to photograph faces, as they say in the trade.

As the funeral got under way again I realised that the little chapel in Manor Park would hold about 60 people. I dashed in and was the only reporter there when the priest began his few words. In those days Catholic funerals followed a pretty set pattern and he opened up with Latin.

Never had my schoolboy Latin worked so hard. The gist of his message was that *'If there were any present with thoughts of vengeance in their minds let them put such thoughts aside and realise how our Lord taught forgiveness...'*

When I got out of the service the Fleet Street pack jumped on me. 'What did he say..what did he say?'

'Hang on guys, it was in Latin but I'll give it to you in a moment.'

I was covering the event not just for the *Independent* but also the *News Chronicle* and had taken the precaution of arranging to use a nearby householder's phone for a couple of quid. I doubt if there was a public phone box in the East End that worked and mobiles were not known, even in science fiction.

After teasing the pack with a couple of sentences in Latin I gave them my intro on the lines of *if there be any here with thoughts of vengeance in their hearts etc.* Nearly every national newspaper used that line.

On Saturday afternoons it was my job to cover Leyton Orient, managed by the wily Alec Stock. I got story after story from Alec and travelled with the team to away games. Inevitably we would meet at Euston or Kings Cross and he would wave at me: 'We've got your ticket, m'son.' Everybody was m'son to Alec.

He had been a tank commander during World War II and there were few better people at understanding men. But we had one colossal row.

Orient were looking certain to get a £30,000 loan from Leyton council to improve their ground when they sold Vic Groves, a centre forward, for £30,000 to Arsenal. Alec had signed him for next to nothing from Walthamstow Avenue.

Once more, struggling for a lead story I put a different spin on the transfer. The tenure of my article was that as Orient had raised this huge sum from the sale of Groves and Stan Charlton they wouldn't need the council loan. After all, the council really didn't have £30,000 to spare with 14,000 people still on the housing waiting list.

On Tuesday morning, my regular call to Orient, I strolled in to be met by Alec who was in a fury. 'How dare you come in here after writing that story,' he shouted. From there on the row escalated.

'You tell me one fact in that story which is wrong,' I shouted back. Office staff and players melted away as we raged on. Within 48 hours all was forgotten and forgiven. We were mates again.

Not only that but Alec was to come to my rescue.

As an editor Dick Harold was hard but pretty fair. Not so the managing director, (known as Mr Leonard) one of a family that owned the *Independent* and 28 other local newspapers in the London area. Two car dealers who owned a massive showroom on Leytonstone High Street had opened an oyster bar and according to Harold, Mr Leonard Locks, a director, had decided that I was the man to write a feature on it, really just a big puff to support their advertising.

I went along to the showroom twice but on each occasion they were patronising and 'too busy to talk to you at the moment. Come back later.' To be rebuffed twice was enough in my book and I ignored them.

Harold took exception to my attitude and insisted, 'Mr Leonard particularly wants you to do this story.'

'In that case, I quit.' I put it rather more rudely, with a suggestion about what Mr Leonard could do with his job. That was, of course, an anatomical impossibility.

Came the Tuesday morning for my last call on Orient when I told Alec he would not be seeing me again as I was leaving the *Independent.* 'You going to Fleet Street?'

'I wish...no and I haven't got another job yet.' I told him the story.

Alec then introduced me to Tom Bailey, the editor of the *Stratford Express,* and that is how I moved from being a reporter to a sub editor on Britain's biggest circulation local paper.

There was one, tiny, weeny problem. I knew little about subbing. Fortunately Mike Gabbert, who had moved to Stratford as a sub from reporting in Walthamstow, spent an afternoon with me in a Lyons coffee house marking my card and teaching me the basics. At the same time I signed on for evening classes, two nights a week, at the London School of Printing in Camberwell. The course included page design and typography that put me ahead of most of my contemporaries.

That was a fair exchange for Mike was moving to the London Bureau of the Associated Press of America. The AP was – and still is - the great rival to the British agency Reuters. I had been there for an unsuccessful trial but knew exactly what they wanted and had briefed Mike.

Deadlines all my Life

CHAPTER 4

My foray into sub-editing

The *Stratford Express* published three editions and I was responsible for the Leyton one. In addition I continued to cover Leyton Orient for Sports Editor Harry Miller, later to become a top football writer for the *Daily Mirror*. He handled West Ham. In return for my Saturday afternoon I got Thursday afternoon off after the paper came off the Press at 1p.m. Little did I know, then, that all the staff got Thursday afternoon off.

Strange how you remember your mistakes rather than triumphs. One of my early page headlines concerned Hannen Swaffer, the renowned columnist on the *Sunday People*. Sorensen had clashed vehemently with Swaffer over reform to the mental health act.

Swaff published a vitriolic riposte to Sorensen's proposed amendments and this was a good page lead for the Leyton edition. My headline read: *Sorensen's mental health bill sends Swaffer raving mad.* Clever stuff.

Came Tuesday morning and a letter arrived from the *People* lawyers pointing out this gross libel on their distinguished columnist. The editor dropped the letter on my desk with the suggestion that I had better sort it out: that is, if I wanted to keep my job. I rang Swaff and asked if I could call on him on Thursday afternoon. He agreed.

I was shown up to his office in Long Acre and said how sorry I was and realised it was a stupid headline. How could I put things right?

'Well, you won't do it again, will you?'

'No sir.'

'Well you can help me sort these letters out.'

Stacked around the office three feet high were piles of letters from readers. The only person I knew who got a post like that was a year or two later when I glimpsed the volume of mail generated by the *Mirror's* agony aunt, Marje Proops.

So I spent the afternoon opening Swaff's mail, sorting out the wheat from the chaff and learning a huge amount from the old master as he chatted on nonstop with anecdote after anecdote. He had been a favourite of Lord Northcliffe and editor of the *Sunday Dispatch* in his prime.

On other Thursday afternoons I worked as a judge at Hackney Wick greyhound stadium.

This arose from a chance meeting with the manager who wanted somebody to take pictures of the dogs for their owners. I still had my trusty Zorki and charged £1 a time and 25p for an 8 x 6inch print. It was all done on a

52

Sunday morning. Suddenly I had a cheque for £150 and shot around to the local department store with June to buy her two dresses: a blue needle cord velvet job with a white bow and a red and white candy-striped shirtwaister. She looked wonderful.

The rest went on a beaten up 1938 Triumph Dolomite that I bought from a compositor for £115.

After taking the pictures, which became a steady earner in local parlance, Hackney asked if I could work part-time on Thursday afternoons which is how I became a judge at London's biggest centre for the needy and greedy. It was a far cry from Walthamstow, showpiece of greyhound racing.

The old Dolomite, which figured largely in our lives, needed some tlc. I ran it up two scaffold planks balanced on oil drums on a bombsite opposite our flat and began to dismantle the engine, holding the manual in one hand and a spanner or screwdriver in the other. The head and other parts were taken into our kitchen, when our landlady was out, and placed on newspaper. June never thought the car would go again for I was not renowned as an engineer.

However, I gave it a de-coke, new valve springs and valves. Ground them in, put it together and it roared away down the Southend road. We were mobile.

Jim Ashford had by now forsaken his South African girl friend and returned to Devon to run one of his father's cafes and holiday apartments in Woolacombe.

He used to ring up from time to time and say: 'Father's had a cancellation. If you can get down here you can have one of the flats.'

If the Dolomite could go around the block we would set off. It always got us there but we often had adventures and roadside repairs on the return trip. There were no motorways to make life easy.

Jim's corner café had an ice cream window for holidaymakers. The resort was so safe Howard could wander off and inevitably turn up with a huge ice cream cornet.

'Where did you get that?'

'Uncle Jim.'

We dined in the café and Jim's mother and father would not take payment. At the end of the week Jim would reluctantly say: 'OK, give us a tenner to put in the till.' This barely covered the picnic that Mrs Ashford used to prepare for our return journey.

Apart from weekends in Bournemouth to see our parents this was our only holiday. Stratford was ok but I missed the buzz of reporting. On one occasion the editor could not think of a subject for a leader. I knew we were raising the price of the paper by a penny and promptly wrote one for him, quoting how the price of newsprint had risen from £x to £y a ton and how the paper had maintained the same price for five years and gave the finest local news service for the greatest public. When the chairman, Stanley Wilson, arrived for his weekly chat with the editor there was much discussion as they read the leader and a few nods in my direction, visible through the glass partition. On his way out Wilson, who was painfully shy, nodded and smiled at me.

I was not to know it at the time but that 300-word leader was to change my life. Unknown to Stratford, and everybody else except Mike Gabbert, I had visited AP for another trial shift and had been promised the next job. Before that came up I had applied for a sports sub's job on the *Evening Standard*. The Sports Editor, Peter Goodall, gave me a searching interview involving football, rugby, cricket, racing and boxing but said, 'I don't see how anybody from a weekly paper can work at the pace required on an evening paper in London.'

'Well, I have Thursday afternoons off and I'll come up and work a trial for four afternoons to show you that I can. If I can't, then goodbye and no hard feelings.' We shook hands and that was my first job in Fleet Street.

After a week or so I found I was handling racing. It became apparent that this was the job nobody else on the sports desk wanted. There was a vast amount of work for the racing edition special, due off the Press at 9a.m. and changes throughout the day for seven subsequent editions. Goodall was little help. On Saturdays he insisted on doing the layouts himself and he wasn't that good. Inevitably he tried to cram too much in the available space leaving me to sort it out on the stone with the printers. Goodall would then appear on the stone (the print shop) look at the mess and offer his standard opinion: 'You fucked that up cocky didn't you.' And walk away. This meant a frantic re-jig to get the Classified edition with all the football and racing results on the street in competition with the *Evening News* and *Star*. Luckily I had two compositors, Sid and Ron, who worked like lightning as I trimmed a paragraph here and re-jigged a story there, often just reading from the type.

I used to get home exhausted but Howard would be watching for me from our upstairs flat window. He would race down the road and jump into my arms. Then we would play football with a big beach ball in our lounge. That kept me sane. Mrs Advice, our landlady, who lived downstairs, never uttered a word of complaint.

At the time London had three evening papers: the *Standard*, the *News* and the *Star*, all paid-for and selling around 2.5million copies each evening.

After a month I found I could handle everything thrown at me and deal with Goodall who topped the league for the most unpopular man in Fleet Street. That was a very competitive league. I was paid £19 a week, £1 over the union minimum because Beaverbrook said that none of his journalists worked for the minimum rate. Consequently, after paying tube fares and going out for a bite of lunch I was no better off than I had been at Stratford.

That was to change. I drew an extra £3 for getting in at 7.30a.m.rather than 8a.m. because of the work load on racing, and covered minor boxing shows during two evenings a week for another £7. One venue I covered was Walworth Road Baths where my father had boxed as an amateur.

Then the *Sunday Express* sports desk, which like all Sundays, augmented its tiny regular staff with people doing shifts on Saturday evenings, were short one day and Gus Hines, a fine cricketer and colleague, suggested me and I walked down the street to the black Lubyanka as the *Express* building in Fleet Street was known. That was another fiver.

As Warren Buffet was to say on a later occasion with slightly different figures, a million here, a million there and soon you're talking real money.

Bill Smith, the Sports Editor, welcomed me as did his deputy Les Vanter who had been one of my predecessors at the Standard, and handed me over to

George Breach, also an ex Standard man who had walked out when Goodall was made Sports Editor. George was currently Sports Editor of the *Daily Sketch*, a county class chess player, a wonderful raconteur and a fine journalist with a strong West Country burr untouched by 30 years in London.

'Know anything about cricket?' he growled. I was up and running, subbing my idol Denis Compton, who was covering a Test Match in South Africa. I had covered Denis in one of his last county matches. He had turned out for Middlesex against Essex for Dickie Dodds' benefit match. By then, thanks to an old knee injury received while playing football for Arsenal, Denis could only walk singles and certainly not run twos or threes. Such was his magnetism however, he had a huge following which boosted the gate and receipts for Dickie. Denis obliged with a ton. As I reported, form is temporary, class is permanent. I was the first reporter to reveal that Dickie, a devout Christian, gave the total proceeds of his benefit match to Moral Re-Armament.

As first edition time approached there was no copy from Denis and George handed me the agency reports and said, ' You'd better use that and put his name on it.' So I did. For 14 years I worked on the *Sunday Express* one day a week, subbing on the sports desk and reporting on cricket and football.

Meanwhile we had moved from Leytonstone to a beautiful wooden bungalow and garden situated in the grounds of a farmhouse in Old Coulsdon, Surrey. It was idyllic and wonderful for Howard.

Another memory sticks in my mind from the *Standard*. George Whiting was a brilliant writer on boxing and missed an interview with an American boxer arriving in Southampton from the United States on the Queen Elizabeth. George, ever resourceful, interviewed an American actress instead – as if she were a boxer. This so tickled Beaverbrook that he rang the editor, Percy Elland, to ensure he would make greater use in future of Whiting's talent. Indeed he would. Elland was no fool. George was paired with Jak, a talented cartoonist and the two produced some great copy.

One day George returned from America where he had been covering a world title fight. He sat at the end of a long desk where I was toiling away. I was shouting Boy! A copy boy would appear, take the sheets of edited paper and stuff them down a chute to the composing room.

George was also shouting Boy! And one would appear. Instead of his sheets going to the printer they were going up to accounts. George was doing his expenses from his American trip. Eventually a little man in a grey suit appeared and coughed deferentially behind George's chair to gain his attention.

Whiting deigned to acknowledge his presence.
'Excuse me George, it says here that you are charging an air fare from San Francisco to Los Angeles for a possible

feature on Jean Simmons. While you were in America Jean Simmons was in England.'

'Really,' said George reaching for his pen. 'Better make it Liz Taylor, then.'

'OK, George,' said the little man and returned upstairs. Oh, to be a super star!

After eight months on the Standard, AP rang me. There was a vacancy on the UK desk. Was I still interested?

Sure. I was desperate to get back to news, preferably before I punched Goodall.

I handed in my notice expecting to be released in a month but my contract stated that three months' notice was required and the *Standard* were not going to let me off the hook. Suddenly, in the eyes of Goodall, I went from bum of the month to Mr Indispensable.

I went back to Don McNicol, UK desk editor who said they could not keep the job open that long. AP operated a three-shift system – 8a.m.to 4p.m. then 4p.m. to midnight and midnight to 8a.m. Could I work the 4p.m. to midnight while I served out my notice at the *Standard?* The idea appealed to McNicol. He was also prepared to organise the rota to allow me to continue at the *Sunday Express* on Saturdays.

For three months I worked around 88 hours a week and at the end of the time bought my first decent car, an Austin A50, outright for cash: £535.

June protected my occasional bouts of sleep like a tigress. Not even our landlord was allowed to mow the lawn if I had my head down.

But there was a mystery about the cottage that took time to solve. When Howard appeared early in the morning in our bedroom his pyjama bottoms were often wet around the ankles. He wouldn't say why.

Then we discovered that as soon as he woke up he would open a window and tumble head first out onto the dew-laden lawn and play away happily. But he could not climb back in. He had to stay outside until the paper girl arrived and she lifted him up and popped him back through the window.

Deadlines all my Life

CHAPTER 5

The highs and lows of family life

By the late 1950s two events happened in quick succession. My parents' marriage was over and it had not been the happiest times for either of them. My earliest memory is of my mother walking out on my father and him sending me running down the road to get her back. I was four years old. The marriage creaked away until the war years when he joined the Royal Navy in 1940. Absence did not make the hearts grow fonder but it meant less upheaval and fewer rows.

Before he left for the navy my father was determined that I should learn to swim. As soon as I could splash across two widths at the local baths he was happy.

During the war years, horse-drawn vehicles seemed to deliver everything: coal, bread, milk and even lemonade. When the coalman came my mother asked me to stand at the front gate and count the number of bags the coalman delivered. The poor man had to hump in 20 x one-hundredweight bags to make up the ton that lasted us through the winter. If any of these delivery horses left a 'calling card' in the road I was sent out with shovel and bucket to collect the manure that was then dug into the garden. You had to be quick because other householders would be on the look out for this bonus.

The end of World War II was greeted with relief and celebrations. Practically every street held a party for children. We gazed in wonder at jellies, tinned fruit, cakes and cream as if they were gifts from another planet. Every mother had decided to raid her special store. Even the corner grocery store that adhered strictly to the ration book allowance, weighed in with special, free offerings which had been 'under the counter,' for years.

Fireworks, canon crashers and jumping jacks, which had been in store for six years, were on sale at corner shops but sweets and chocolate were still rationed.

At our early scout camps rationing was still in progress and we had to take our own share of provisions. Once more the local shop seemed to provide excellent supplements from a secret store.

Scout camps were magical in my eyes: freedom under the watchful eyes of Captain Brough, our group scoutmaster, and his assistant Ron. Their planning and efforts meant so much to us boys in those simple times.

A few months later my father returned home to Bournemouth and for weeks seemed content to do nothing. He took me to football (Arsenal v Chelsea), cricket (Hampshire v Yorkshire), racing (Bath,

Goodwood and Salisbury), the theatre, music hall and around London. It was a great time.

All seemed well and I passed the 11 plus in 1946 and went to Bournemouth Grammar School. I joined the army cadets and then transferred to the naval section with 'camps' aboard HMS Duke of York, a WWII decommissioned battleship moored in Portsmouth Harbour and used for cadet training.

As soon as we cadets were aboard we went to the ship's shop and bought HMS Duke of York hatbands that we substituted for Bournemouth School CCF as soon as we were ashore. We were not to know that this gentle introduction to service life would help us later on for National Service. The navy were masters at enforcing a modicum of discipline while turning a blind eye to some of our antics. The chief petty officers had been handpicked for the job.

Sport was high on the agenda at Bournemouth School and to get into the school cricket or football teams needed a competitive spirit. I think my parents wished that I had shown the same ambition for examinations. Being the rebel and joker in the class seemed more attractive.

My father went back to sea, this time not to the Royal Navy but with Cunard, sailing aboard the old Aquitania and the Queen Mary. He was seldom at home which was a relief from the tension and rows.

My mother and I had seen little of him after I joined the army at 18 and by the time I returned he was gone for good and a divorce took place.

As a result, my mother, one of a family of 15, sold her home and joined her brother Tom who had taken a pub, The Bull, in Salisbury next to the hospital. She did all the cooking – homemade pasties and bar food, apart from generally helping out. All she received was her keep. Tom, it's correct to say, was not my favourite uncle.

On a visit to see my mother, June and I found her in her room in tears. She was exhausted from overwork and looked terrible. June helped her to pack a couple of cases with her clothes and we left. I met Tom in his bar. 'Mother's leaving.'

'What's the problem?' he blustered and wisely retreated behind the bar.

We had a spare room at our wooden cottage and she soon recovered. In June and Howard she found love and in turn thought the world of them. To maintain that happy state and equilibrium we decided that we needed a bigger place and about two miles away found a good, unfurnished detached house to rent: 20 Coulsdon Road. I turned the smallest bedroom into a kitchenette for my mother who had the large bedroom as a bed sitting room. It worked well and she even found a part-time job at a hotel in Croydon as a housekeeper.

Howard, although only four years old, was so adventurous that we decided to see if he could begin school. There was a little private school within half a mile where the headmistress was Miss Martin. We three trooped into her elegant drawing room to be interviewed. June and I were on tenterhooks, not because we felt she would refuse him but because we feared he would knock over one of the delightful china ornaments she had around the room.

Miss Martin stayed quite calm, however, as he wandered around, and agreed he could attend morning classes. That didn't last long. After a month he wanted to stay all day.

At the school's Christmas pantomime he got the biggest laugh of the day. On stage, waiting for the performance to begin, he walked to the edge and looked down at June, one of several mothers perched on school chairs. 'Mum! You forgot to sew this button on,' pointing to a gap in his clean white shirt.

As we were both only children we didn't want Howard to be in that category. While I was at AP the Bureau chief offered me the chance to transfer to the New York Office. This was a huge step up. I would be on the American rate which was treble the £24 a week I was getting in London.

Home I went completely thrilled. 'I've got news for you,' I burst out, handing over a bunch of flowers in the first stage of a celebration.

'And I've got news for you,' she replied. 'I'm pregnant again.' We were thrilled, but New York would have to wait. The flowers marked a different celebration.

We had moved home on several occasions and it was time to buy a property. The Coulsdon/Purley area suited us fine and we searched every spare minute. Apart from Howard we now had Linnie and Beanie. I was to learn how daft fathers could be facing the wiles of small daughters. They had their brother and me totally at their command. They were extra fuel for my ambition.

We found a five-bedroomed, detached house (4 Valley Road, Kenley, Surrey) with about a quarter of an acre garden. It had once boasted a tennis court and orchard but these had been hived off by the new owners who planned to build two chalet bungalows.

The house had been requisitioned by the R.A.F. during the war and needed a great deal of work. Kenley had been one of the front line airfields for fighters in the Battle of Britain. Getting a mortgage was a nightmare. I think we were turned down four times despite the fact that I had a more than adequate income. The price for the property was £4250 and each mortgage application set me back the cost of a survey fee and valuation. I took a builder friend around the property and asked for his view. 'Just scrape together every penny you can even if it means you have no furniture and have to sit on orange boxes,' was his advice.

Eventually we got a mortgage from the local authority, Coulsdon and Purley Urban District Council. The rate was a quarter per cent over the usual amount but was fixed at six and one eighth per cent and could go neither up nor down during a 25-year term. It turned out to be the deal of a lifetime. Then a last-minute snag threatened our purchase.

The developers insisted that we should buy half of what had been an architect's single-storey studio extension for another £250. The deal was in the melting pot but June's parents came to the rescue and her mother arrived with £250 in notes. Our half of the studio became a garage.

The deal was done...despite evidence of dry rot, rising damp and woodworm. The lender retained £300 until the woodwork and dry rot had been eradicated.

For six months I spent every spare moment with a paintbrush or tools in my hands, while my building contact had his men install a solid fuel central heating system and others repaired plaster. Friends also pitched in to help us, notably Bill Chiles, one of my old Leyton team who was always welcome in our home and another honorary uncle for Howard.

June proved to be adept at paper hanging and that was a big plus. Was there no end to the girl's talents?

I continued working at AP and would rate Don McNicol as one of the best re-write men I ever worked with. Every cable had to be meticulously written for the

British Press with no Americanisms allowed and fact after fact attributed. The AP said nothing; all views were attributed to a source. Mike Gabbert was also highly regarded and stood in for McNicol as desk editor.

I fared well apart from one blunder. Strange how these are fresher in the mind than triumphs. President Eisenhower was involved with some international crisis and put forward his six-point plan for peace. As it came in line by line I edited it and shoved it out to the teleprinter operator as fast as I could go.

On the way home I bought the London evening papers. All of them had carried my AP story with the headline: *Ike's six-point peace plan.* Strangely they only carried five of the points. Two of them were so similar I had run them into one but nobody seemed over worried. The evening papers also worked at pace.

By accident I also became AP's cricket correspondent and each week several newspapers in the West Indies carried my by-lined round-up of the county cricket matches. American Eddy Gilmore was an AP star, who had won the coveted Pulitzer Prize for outstanding journalism and he decided to write a piece on cricket. Eddy was straight out of central casting. Sat in the office, complete with red braces, chomping on a cigar, his four-finger typing rapped out copy with the speed and noise of an AK47. He had been Moscow correspondent, survived a honey trap and smuggled out his Russian, ballerina

70

wife. If you can get his book: *Me and My Russian Wife*, it's a great read.

To write his piece on cricket he fired questions across the huge AP office to me. 'Hey John, is it true they stop for lunch? And tea?' Each of my answers was followed by a guffaw and another four-finger burst on the trigger.

Another notable journalist and author to appear at AP was David Eliades. He had escaped from Cyprus where he was on an EOKA hit list.

David had worked for the *Times of Cyprus*, an English-language newspaper edited and owned by British journalist Charles Foley. Like all good newspapers it upset both the British government and the EOKA rebels. David, a great guy to have at a party, later joined the *Sunday Express* as Foreign Editor and also wrote several successful novels and plays with Bob Forrest.

Frequently Mike, David and I would meet others of a similar ilk – Herbie Kretzmer and Les Thomas - at the Pickwick Club in Charing Cross Road very late on a Saturday night. They had a good little group called the Pedlars, awful food before midnight and good breakfasts after 4a.m. June used to drive up from Kenley to meet me as I finished the late shift on the *Sunday Express* at 11p.m. If we didn't go to the Pickwick we caught a late night film or dinner at Chez Solange, one of our favourite restaurants.

All, or most, was about to change.

Deadlines all my Life

CHAPTER 6

Exclusive stories and lawyers

My old boss at the *Stratford Express*, Jim Amer, the Managing Director, invited me to lunch at the Devonshire just off the Strand. He asked what I was doing. How would I like to re-join the *Stratford Express* and *Romford Times* as assistant to him and chairman Stanley Wilson? I would learn the business of newspaper management.

The salary was a move up from what I was earning, the prospects were considerable and the company needed an infusion of younger ideas. In time I would become a director and succeed Amer when Wilson retired. It was a tempting prospect. But I was still young and found journalism in all its aspects a great job. Did I really want to give that up?

June and I talked it over and decided it was too good an opportunity to miss. Stanley Wilson had clearly marked me down as a cut above the usual journalist, all because of that leader I had written on newsprint prices. I said goodbye to the AP but kept my Saturday job on the

73

Sunday Express, not just for the cash, but also as a link to what I enjoyed doing.

A couple of stories spring to mind. I was covering Chelsea against Ipswich, one managed by Dave Sexton and Ipswich by Bobby Robson.

Alan Hudson smashed a shot from just outside the area and the ball flew past a goalpost to hit the stanchion holding up the net and rebounded into play. The referee signalled a goal and it stood despite protests from the Ipswich players and an incandescent Bobby Robson. I returned to the *Sunday Express* office to find my story being pored over by the tame lawyer brought in for a Saturday evening session. 'Is this true,' he asked. 'Are you sure?'

Very early in my days on the *Daily Express* the managing editor had told me that lawyers were there to advise not to instruct. Before I could reply the picture editor appeared with a superb shot of the incident showing clearly the ball did not go into goal. Another back page lead.

Then to Fulham one sunny Saturday afternoon where Johnny Haynes was a genius among a host of lesser characters. Midway through the second half with Fulham having squandered pass after defence-splitting pass from Haynes he clearly had had enough of his colleagues and walked off the pitch signalling a substitute to go on. Nobody else seemed to twig it. Haynes was certainly not injured. Substitutes had only just been introduced to the

English leagues and he was definitely not ordered on by the manager.

After the game I waited until other Press colleagues had departed and challenged Bill Dodgin the manager. 'Johnny quit, didn't he, Bill?' Now Bill was not one of those managers who would or even could lie. 'Well, he had a bit of an ankle,' said Bill. I challenged him again and he just walked away.

I couldn't get Haynes himself so filed the story saying that the Johnny Haynes, the first £100 a week footballer, had quit in the middle of a game.

Back at the office the same lawyer was peering at my copy. 'Did anybody else see this?' he asked.

'Only 25,000 people in the crowd.'

'Is this story true?'

Murder in the Newsroom would be a good title for a detective story. Except there would have been no mystery.

Bill Dodgin would neither confirm nor deny my story when telephoned and then Tommy Trinder, the comedian and chairman of Fulham F.C. telephoned and spoke to John Junor, the Editor, saying he would sue the paper if we printed the story. Big mistake. 'Back page lead,' said Junor. Page lead stories are like a shot of adrenalin to reporters.

I enjoyed working as a sports reporter for the *Sunday Express* and while I never matched the prose heights of Hugh McIlvanney, Ian Wooldridge or Geoffrey Green, nor the encyclopaedic contacts of Norman Giller, Harry Miller, Peter Corrigan or Jim Mossop, I survived by sheer enthusiasm and energy as a substitute for talent. Except that is, for one occasion.

I was down to cover an FA cup-tie at Crystal Palace who were drawn against Barnsley. Alongside me were Norman Giller, covering for the *Daily Herald* and Don Woodward for the *Daily Express*.

I was asked to file my report direct to Manchester for their first edition as soon as the final whistle blew. In the last seconds Barnsley got a penalty that forced a draw and a replay in Yorkshire.

I whizzed out to the phones that were in a room behind the press box as soon as the final whistle went and adlibbed my intro on how the last-minute penalty had earned a replay for Barnsley.

By the time I arrived downstairs for what passed as a Press Conference in those days Barnsley were heading back north and Bert Head, the Palace manager, was nowhere to be seen.

I had my car and gave Norman and Don a lift back to London, dropping them off at a Tube station. In the office I polished my report for the London edition and went home.

All was well until Monday morning when I opened the *Express* and bought the *Herald*. Both carried identical back page leads that nobody else had. *Referee Books 10 Palace Players*, then a record.

Apparently Steve Kember, the Palace skipper, had protested at the penalty award and as the match official walked off the pitch had lined up his players as a sarcastic guard of honour to applaud the referee saying words to the effect: 'Let's hear it for the ref. Best player for Barnsley.'

The only reason the referee did not book the goalkeeper was because he was still on his way to join the guard of honour and did not take part.

I rang Norman at the *Herald.* 'I'm so sorry Johnny. I asked Don what we should do about you.' With great economy, Don had replied. 'F*** him. He's got his last-minute penalty and story, we need something new for Monday morning.'

'Don't worry, Norman,' I said. 'I'd have done the same to you.' A few months later he was chief football writer for the *Daily Express.*

On another occasion I had to file a quick report to the *Sunday Express* when Spurs were playing Manchester United. I got through to the copytaker and insisted that I would dictate the teams first and he should get that away. The report would be given to him in short takes that should be sent immediately to the sports desk for onward transmission to Manchester.

Often these guys could be difficult and it paid to be firm with them. I told him not to interrupt and get on with it as I wanted to catch united players and officials before they departed. At the close I put down the phone and raced towards the dressing room in the hope of getting a reasonable quote or two.

Later I drifted back to the *Sunday Express* to see a few grinning faces around the sports subs' desk. 'Good game, John?' Said the Sports Editor. 'Yes, I replied, ' could make a back page lead.'

'Did you have a drink there?'

'Yes, I did.'

'Did you have two drinks?'

'Yes, as a matter of fact I did.'

'Good,' he replied and walked off.

By this time the grins had broken out into outright laughter. I had only filed my story to the *Sunday Telegraph* by mistake.

They had rung the *Sunday Express* sports desk and asked if they were expecting a report from John Jenkins.

'Well, if you like to send somebody round you can collect it. But tell him, please, not to bollock our copytakers.' I never lived that down

* * * *

I spent around three months as Amer's assistant. He knew a great deal about management but little about newspapers. He had begun life as a printer, got a commission in the Royal Navy during the war and progressed to his current position. The group had two newspapers, five stationery shops and a jobbing printing works, largely dependent on orders from the Ford motor company. We used to tour each centre once a week and later Amer would send me off on my own. It was a steep but interesting learning curve. I worked out the commission for the advertising managers, ordered in newsprint and ink, checked over management books with a cheerful accountant called Walker and tried hard to bite my tongue on what I saw was wrong with the newspapers where sales were declining. There was no doubt that the newspapers, packed solid with pre-paid classified advertising, were cash cows.

In an attempt to revive circulations the group decided to replace both editors. I was given the task of advertising for replacements. We had 187 replies, whittled them down to 10 and presented the chairman with six. He didn't like any of them.

After a good deal of soul searching, and not discussing my decision with anybody, I told Amer that I would like to apply for the job as editor of the *Stratford Express*. I admitted that I would be unlikely to stay for another three or four years in my present role as I missed being a journalist.

He and Wilson agreed I could have a three-month trial in the job. If I failed I would have to leave and could not transfer back to management. I raced home to give June the good news. She smiled. She was not in the least surprised. I was 24 years old and the next three years were going to be some ride.

Deadlines all my Life

CHAPTER 7

An editor in the East End

It would be fair to say that the editorial staff of the *Stratford Express* viewed my appointment with more than grave misgivings. I was either a management nark, I was too young for the job or I had all the faults one picked up in Fleet Street which would spell death for a sound, local paper. Some would say there was much truth in these claims.

I spent the first day interviewing them individually. A few seemed happy, some were distinctly unhappy and most reserved judgment. In my first month I released four as humanely as possible. I told them to look around for another job. If after a month they had not found one I would give them a month's notice.

For the rest of my three-year tenure as editor I sacked only two people and one confessed to me later that it was the best thing that had ever happened to her as 'she needed a kick up the arse.'

I hired Roger Windsor, who was desperate to get a start in journalism after being secretary to the Sports Editor of the *Evening Standard*, and Paul Thomas from

Leyton Independent days who had joined me there from school. Stuart Griffiths, a graduate from Oxford, added gravitas to the staff and later became a leader writer on the *Evening Standard.* Finally Mike Williams, cruelly sacked by the *Standard* in the week he was married, came aboard as news editor. The team was complete.

They were a great bunch and soon morphed into a solid team. I told them that not only were we the biggest local paper in the land we were also going to be the best. Seeing the number of mistakes which appeared in the early editions that claim was difficult to prove.

My reporters were razor keen but sometimes wickedly careless on details. In desperation I required them to sign every story under a sentence saying:

All names, addresses and facts checked. If a mistake occurred after that, they faced instant dismissal. I never had to carry out the threat and accuracy improved all round.

The paper established an astonishing reputation and I lost many members of staff to Fleet Street which, with no justification at all, irked me greatly. Harry Miller went to the *Mirror,* Mike Williams joined the *Telegraph* and others found greener pastures at home and abroad. Replacements included Norman Giller as Sports Editor, a hugely talented writer whom I lured back from *Boxing News* for another ten bob a week, Al Shillum later to become managing editor of the *Mirror* and Tony Clifton, an Aussie who became one of the last reporters to leave

Vietnam. There was also Phyl Procter, daughter of the legendary Harry Procter of tabloid fame. She could have doubled for Brigitte Bardot, and a blue and white check mini-dress did nothing to contradict that view.

Phyl had walked out of the *Woman's Mirror* after refusing to get her hair permed. Their loss, my gain. Each week I insisted that Phyl should be off the diary and sent out to find a story. She never let me down and filed some crackers. One concerned a lady in Stratford market who had worked her butt off running a fruit and veg stall. She had saved for years to buy a fur coat. Together with Phyl, a carrier bag full of 2000 one-pound notes, and a photographer she went shopping up West as they used to say in our manor. Not to Harrods or Harvey Nicks but behind Oxford Street where you could get twice the value for a full-length mink coat. To the chagrin of my staff Phyl married a reporter from the PA, thus ending a dozen dreams.

The East End was buzzing. A reporter could gain more experience there in six months than three years anywhere else. Thursday was wage snatch day, Saturday night was break-in time for radio and TV shops, every day was pay-out day for used car dealers, victims of the Krays protection racketeering and Stratford Magistrates court was the busiest in the land.

In sport we had the rise and rise of Orient while the incomparable Bobby Moore, Geoff Hurst and Martin

Peters were making names for themselves at West Ham as a prelude to World Cup glory for England.

We launched the Hammer of the Year competition and the first winner was the centre half Ken Brown. He was a great clubman and earned one cap for England. We arranged for Jimmy Hill, then general secretary of the Players Union, to present his award and that was the first occasion I met Bobby Moore. Sports Editor Harry Miller introduced us and Bobby was among a clutch of young West Ham hopefuls attending the event in club blazers, smart shirts and club ties. All those players who attended were a credit to the club and the game.

A few years later I covered a game in which Geoff Hurst scored six goals when West Ham beat Sunderland 8 - 0. Interviewing Geoff at the end of the game he told me that he put the first one in with his hand and it should have been disallowed.

'You know what you are saying, Geoff?'

'Yes John, but I was not to know I'd get another five. Last week I had a perfectly good goal disallowed at Southampton.'

Another back page lead. Strange to say the BBC, and David Coleman, ducked the story and after many years Geoff traced a film of the match.

Boxing had always been big in the East End and Billy Walker, won the British (ABA) Amateur Heavyweight title. Soon after a first-round knockout of 6 ft. 4 in American champion Cornelius Perry in an international televised tournament, promoters were queuing up to sign him. Managed by his brother George, a more than useful cruiserweight, he retired at 30, a wealthy man.

Then there were the exploits of Terry Spinks and Sammy McCarthy. You could often find them in The Two Puddings opposite our office in Stratford Broadway. Terry won a gold medal at the Olympics before becoming British champion featherweight, while Sammy's fight with Dave Charnley from Dartford truly deserves the overused words, epic encounter.

We were also a crusading paper, reporting on one lady Labour councillor who had moved four times, on each occasion to a new council house while our contacts gave us a lead which landed an ex government minister in jail for four years.

It began with a mother calling into our office to say she was worried about a man who was giving her little boy a lot of money and taking him for rides in his car.

After some brilliant investigative reporting led by Shillum, and overcoming some threats and obstacles put in our way, Sir Ian Horobin admitted ten charges of assault in July 1962, and was sentenced to four years imprisonment.

Politics were also lively and I enjoyed the company of Arthur Lewis and Elwyn Jones who were our local Members of Parliament. They often entertained me to lunch at the Commons.

Arthur was a typical old style TGWU stalwart, lying down in front of lorries when the dockers were picketing the dock gates. Elwyn was a more patrician character, an eminent Q.C. and later Attorney General. I preferred Arthur. 'You can only wear one suit at a time John and you only need three meals a day.' The man was a sage. He had just come back from a trade fair in Eastern Europe where he visited the stand of an East End firm making pocket Geiger counters, rather like bulky fountain pens.

While waiting for Khruschev and his entourage to come around, the Geiger counter man confessed it would be wonderful if Mr K visited his stand.

'Gimmee one of those pens,' said Arthur. As the First Secretary of the USSR approached, Arthur stepped out, introduced himself and gave him one of the 'pens' with a short speech to say he hoped Mr K would only ever have to use it for peaceful purposes. The message was duly translated and as the procession moved on a Soviet acolyte was dispatched to the stand and ordered £20,000 worth.

'Arthur, I really don't know how to thank you,' said Mr Geiger Counter.

'How about two grand?' said Arthur.

Another MP to cross my path was the dishonourable Member for Barking, Tom Driberg. He had been a star columnist - and William Hickey - for Beaverbrook Newspapers before he was sacked by Arthur

Christiansen, the famous *Daily Express* Editor. Driberg had a penchant for biting the hand that fed him. He once publicly denounced the staff on *Express* newspapers as 'wage slaves.'

This came to Beaverbrook's ears who had often bailed him out financially and paid for his defence against accusations of cottaging and rough trade. The Beaver rang Chris. 'If you have any wage slaves, Mr Christiansen, set them free.'

In fact Driberg was charged with indecent assault after an incident in which he had shared his bed with two Scotsmen picked up in London, then a criminal offence. Beaverbrook paid for a leading counsel, J. D. Cassels. Two character witnesses were quickly discovered by the defence. Driberg was acquitted, and Beaverbrook's influence ensured that the case went unreported by the press. This was the first known instance of what Kingsley Amis called the 'baffling immunity Driberg enjoyed from the law and the Press to the end of his days.'

Driberg, who stood for Barking, wrote a column for the now defunct *Reynolds News* and was unwise enough to criticise the *Stratford Express* for being a 'Tory rag.' I picked this up and wrote a direct and an open letter to him, offering him a regular column in the *Stratford Express* to give his viewpoint.

He refused the offer but never again publicly attacked the newspaper. To everybody's surprise we learned that Driberg was to marry. Churchill was among those astonished and was told, she's not a very attractive woman. 'Ah,' said the great man, finding the right words, 'buggers can't be choosers.'

After his death it was widely reported that Driberg was a spy for Russia. It was not something we had the resources to prove or disprove.

I was also to meet another Labour stalwart who had no qualms about accepting money from the right wing press – Woodrow Wyatt. For many years Woodrow wrote a trenchant column for Rupert Murdoch's *News of the World*, was chairman of the Tote and acted as the secret go-between for the newspaper proprietor to Margaret Thatcher. He managed all three tasks with equal flair. He also had a beautiful house next door to Lord's cricket ground and an enviable wine cellar.

At that time West Ham council was 100% Labour and did what they liked. However, a strong Liberal contingent made a concerted attack and won four seats. From then on the council became much more co-operative.

London Docks was also a great source for stories and Jack Dash, their fiery leader, was always ready with a story. One day he called at my office by appointment. He was wearing a beautifully cut mohair suit, crisp white shirt and sober tie.

He opened the conversation. 'Mr Jenkins, we've always co-operated with you and given the *Stratford* some good stories.'

'Indeed you have Jack.'

'And unlike a lot of papers you've always given us a fair crack of the whip.'

'We certainly try Jack.'

'And we've never asked you for anything.'

Here it comes, I thought. 'No, you never have.'

'Well we need a new loud hailer and wondered if you could provide one.'

'No problem, Jack,' and I breathed a sigh of relief. I could easily hide the £40 in my budget. That's how we ran rings around the national papers on stories from dockland.

In show business, Theatre Workshop, the nearest thing to a workers co-operative outside the Soviet Union, flourished under the dynamic influence of Joan Littlewood. It was a golden stepping stone to West End stardom for so many performers, including Barbara Windsor, Yootha Joyce, Tony Booth (Cherie Blair's dad) Victor Spinetti and Harry Corbett. Writers like Brendan Behan and Wolf Mankovitz basked in the glory.

Every summer Joan used to take off for a holiday in Russia. While away on one occasion an actress in the company, the talented Avis Bunnage, moved in with Joan's boyfriend, company manager Gerry Raffles. Despite the fact that Joan herself was married, she was furious.

Gerry, not the strongest character, wailed that Avis would not go when asked to leave. 'Won't she?' said Joan, and promptly threw her rival downstairs.

Other members of my staff did a great job and if I do not remember all their names it is the fault of old age. Paul Thomas became a very good sub, later founding a successful PR agency with a blue chip list of clients, and Roger Windsor graduated from being a sharp reporter to subbing later in life and Night Editor of the *Daily Mail.* I wonder if Paul remembers his early days when he used his bicycle to make calls so he could claim bus fares to eke out his pay?

About that time he founded the Four Ways Car Club in Essex which became an early success as he rallied one of the first Mini Coopers. I occasionally acted as his navigator, a job that demanded nerves of steel as he flung it sideways around corners.

Paul Bach was another talented reporter who was to cross my path again in later years as the outstanding, founding editor of *Saga Magazine*, while Jack Lundin reported and suffered from the horrors he had witnessed in Biafra.

Ronnie Kentish moved over to film publicity with success and Derek Bowman, an Oxford graduate, took an unknown rock star, David Essex, and as agent and mentor turned him into a millionaire.

I should not forget Ivor Davis, a typical cocky, determined East End reporter. He came to me one day and said he was leaving to work as a PR for Butlin's holiday camp. He was going to save all the money he earned and go to America. I told him he was nuts. Off he went and I don't know how many of my staff – and their girl friends - enjoyed free weekends at Butlin's holiday camp in Clacton that year.

At the end of the summer season he turned up to see me before heading for the States. He was going to work his way across America. 'When you get to a town take a story into the local paper editor or radio station and ask for a job for a couple of weeks.' That's how he worked his way west ending up in California on the *Santa Monica Herald*. He even got the editor to commission an article from me. Later Ivor became the man on the west coast for the *Daily Express* and the *Times*. However, he still came back to the UK to get his teeth fixed on the NHS.

A bizarre lead story concerned a greengrocer whose wife dreamt that his dog would win the greyhound Derby. Roger turned in the story which said that the man had mortgaged his business and backed the dog ante post. It had not yet reached the final. He stood to win £30,000, a fortune in those days.

I knew enough about gambling to ask Roger to go back and check the man's betting vouchers. He saw them and it was true.

Roger not only wrote the story but also went down to the local bookies with my tenner and all the change the staff could muster to pile it on Palms Printer. We led the paper on the story and the East End backed it as if there were no tomorrow. Two weeks later Palms Printer won the Greyhound Derby at the White City.

I drove the team hard but they seemed to enjoy life and I still meet Norman, Paul and Roger for lunch a couple of times a year. Norman wrote the scripts for TV's *This is Your Life* for 14 years and has written 109 books. Probably 112 by the time I finish this. Other good guys were Keith Cade, Mr Reliable as a sub, and Ernie McDonald who by sheer hard work earned his spurs. Mac Naughton and Bill Coller, old hands I inherited, sank their prejudices to turn in good performances.

One important cog in the Stratford wheels was my secretary Pat Myers whose owlish spectacles gave a clue to her wisdom. Pat was far from a perfect shorthand typist but she was the kind of gatekeeper that every editor needs.

She had a gift for filtering out time wasters from people I needed to see, marked my card when trouble was brewing from my bunch of pirates masquerading as reporters, and hoisted warning signals when a management storm was brewing.

She would also counsel mercy when I wanted to flog somebody for a minor mistake.

I once said I was lucky to have inherited her – and she replied that was not the case. She had inherited me as she was already in post. She told me that when she had applied to my predecessor for the job she had worn a hat and gloves for the interview. Pat was more South Kensington than Stratford East.

She later became a Research Editor for *Reader's Digest* and proved a valuable ally when my magazine *Raconteur* was the victim of plagiarism.

This occurred when we awarded the *Raconteur* monthly prize of £500 to the alleged author of a beautifully written story that would have been a contender for the big £10,000 annual prize. A letter arrived from a reader saying, among other things, *I thought your stories had to be new and unpublished in any other magazine.*

True. This was a standard requirement in any such competition. In the words of the legal profession I asked my correspondent (a disappointed entrant) *for further and better particulars.*

With substantial prize money available it was – and I suspect still is – possible that desperate people will pass off somebody else's work as their own. My team were pretty good at spotting these, particularly clever clogs who thought that a re-working of a Maupassant or Chekhov, Jack London or an Edgar Allan Poe story would pass muster.

My correspondent replied that she had read a similar story in a Canadian edition of *Reader's Digest.* At the time this magazine was one of the most widely read in the world, published in 17 languages in 27 countries.

I rang Pat Myers. Within a week I had a copy of the Canadian issue containing the story. The story was a theft, which is the best word to describe plagiarism.

Disappointed as I was to lose Pat, and any of my staff, I was quixotically proud of their achievements.

One reporter who never worked for me was the legendary Peter Batt. I did hire him and waited for him to turn up – but he never arrived. Peter could write like an angel and drink like the devil and had been sacked from nearly everywhere. He once showed me a novel threequarters completed and I begged him to finish it, but he never did.

His excuse for not turning up? 'I didn't want to let you down John.' Maybe I was a mug but I actually believed that's how his tortured mind worked. For one of the best of a book full of PB stories we have to fast forward to 1962: a classic Fleet Street record of the unexpected. According to Norman Giller, The Crafty Cockney had blagged his way into a news reporter's job at the *Daily Herald.*

Another sports journalist legend, Colin Hart, later the No 1 boxing reporter, was working as the *Herald*'s night news editor, and when an agency reported that a London-bound plane had crashed in the Pyrenees he sent fireman reporter Batt to the scene. Battman being Battman, he got to the foothills in an inebriated condition, and when the taxi-driver dropped him as close as possible to the scene of the crash, he fell over in the snow semi-conscious while attempting to walk up the mountain.

Rescuers coming down from the wrecked plane found him, picked him up and carried him to a nearby convent where he was put into bed and nursed by nuns, who did not help his condition by giving him copious shots of brandy to warm him up. Word got back to other reporters covering the story that a survivor had been found. They dashed to the convent to discover a pissed-as-a-newt Batty sitting up in bed toasting their arrival and saying: 'Thought I'd died and gorn to 'eaven.'

That was a flashback of my experience of being knocked out on the football field in Austria...but I missed out on the brandy.

About a year after Lin was born along came another daughter: Zena. If there's one thing better than one daughter it's two daughters. Now indeed I had to adopt a more sober and less buccaneering approach to life and career. Apart from editing the *Stratford Express* and Saturday shifting on the *Sunday Express* I was also subbing two nights a week on the *Daily Sketch*. At the time the *Sketch* had two Night Editors who worked on alternate nights. One was a Mancunian whose name I forget. His idea of designing the front page was to pick up a layout pad and scheme in three items: lead, picture and filler, all the time uttering a commentary while drawing the layout. The commentary would go like this,

'We'll have super tit here, pissquick down here and whatsit there.' The chief sub editor, given this decision from on high, would interpret it thus: the picture would either be a well known Royal Shakespeare actress with a plunging neckline or an unknown beach babe in a bikini: pissquick would be an announcement from the Prime Minister or a footballer misbehaving with an actress. Whatsit would be a paragraph on a revolution in a South American country, or a devastating earthquake in Indonesia. Such were the design intricacies of a tabloid front page.

* * * *

June by now had learned to drive and took a part-time job with our dentist, an Australian called Gill Cox, who ran two evening surgeries and looked desperately for nursing help. My mother was only too pleased to babysit for a couple of hours.

One of his patients was a master from Howard's school who offered the view that he had little chance of getting into Dulwich or Whitgift Trinity, our two hopes for his continued education. Silly man. He was the only patient for whom the pain killing injection didn't work.

Stage Two for the improvements in our home included oil-fired central heating, new curtains and carpet, the existing garage converted into a bedroom for

Lin and Zena to share and a car port built to house a caravan and car.

Holidays were spent on the Broads, in Cornwall, Scotland, France and Austria. and the children played a vital role in making life enjoyable for my mother.

Tea with nannie, and a game of gin rummy became their after school ritual, while Howard had excelled by getting a scholarship to Whitgift Trinity. Having passed the entrance examination he faced an interview. We drove up to the school and June accompanied him while I parked the car. As she entered the school in Croydon she was met by a sixth former who said: 'Good afternoon madam, may I take your candidate?' To say she was impressed would be a massive understatement. She handed over her little, brown-eyed candidate with alacrity.

On the way home we quizzed him gently about the interview. One of the questions he was asked concerned cricket. Did he like bowling or batting best?

He thought for a moment and replied: 'Fielding.' Despite a little coaching I never thought of that answer for him. He was in. At that school he became a fine swimmer and athlete, played water polo and made some good friends. He also appeared in a school play. It was very much in the style of an old-fashioned grammar school.

I had taken up golf and on odd afternoons would slope off to Wanstead with Paul where the modest Reg

Knight was a superb teacher. He later co-authored a fine instruction book with an *Express* sub editor, Sid Spicer, called *Learn Golf Backwards*. Reg would teach you to chip and putt first before letting you loose with the driver and other long-range clubs.

Then to our surprise and subsequent delight our fourth child appeared: Sally, the baby of the family. June reckoned six was the ideal family. Howard and I were now truly outgunned. What's better than two daughters? Three daughters.

According to the children one thing was missing from our lives – pets. I did not at that time share the nation's obsession with animals but that was to change. It began with a rabbit, called Hazel Buns and progressed to Frisky, a cat wiser than Solomon, two ponies, (one older than Methuselah) with various successors, and a Dalmatian, Frodo, who had two expressions: puzzled and bewildered. I shared his puzzlement at this turn of events but had seriously underestimated the persuasive power of small girls.

Hazel belonged to everybody and when allowed into the house had to be dissuaded from chewing the TV cables, Frisky belonged to Zena, Frodo was Lin's and the ponies were the joint responsibilities of the girls.

In practise it mostly fell to June and occasionally me to stand in as surrogate carers for this menagerie which later included guinea pigs and a gerbil.

Everything was fine except that after three years as editor of the *Stratford Express* I was fired, told to get out and clear my desk in 20 minutes.

It had been boiling up for a couple of months but with the insouciance of youth I imagined that I was fireproof as the paper was doing very well and we had hoisted the 80,000 sale figure again after it had slipped into the seventies.

My downfall began when I made my m.d. Jim Amer, look a fool in front of his fellow directors who were gathering for a board meeting.

Two of our local coppers had been killed when trying to arrest a gunman and we launched an appeal for the widows. One of the directors asked me how much I thought we would raise and Amer butted into say my total was nonsense.

Moral: never contradict your m.d. in front of his fellow directors and certainly do not add a rider to the effect that he had no idea how much work the editorial team had put into the effort. My forecast was dead on.

Amer's first move was to appoint an editor-in-chief over me. This poor soul, acting under orders, took to poking his nose into my domain and stormed into my office one morning to demand why we were not carrying a certain story that had appeared in one of that week's rival papers. After what could be described as a heated discussion I pointed out that if he read the papers properly he would realise that we had carried it the previous week and the rival paper had picked it up from us.

It's fair to say that I expressed my views in non-Parliamentary language, in fact language more suited to a print shop or stokers' mess, and he stormed off to see Amer. And that was that.

Amer enjoyed his moment of triumph but in retrospect if our positions had been reversed I might well have done the same thing.

Nevertheless, at the ripe old age of 27 I was out of work...for eleven days. Then I had offers from the *Mirror*, the *Sketch* and the *Daily Express*. I chose the latter, under Beaverbrook, probably the best popular newspaper in the world at that time. It sold more copies and had more AB readers than the *Times, Telegraph* and *Guardian* put together.

Then we had a party – a memorable party – for my team at Stratford; visited Harrods to buy June a couple of dresses and went to Woolacombe to see Jim.

My Stratford staff presented me with a pewter tankard inscribed: *From the Stratford Express – as it was,* (in 72pt) the largest typeface I had ever used, and a copy of a resolution they had passed and presented to Amer criticising him for sacking me.

The immediate problem was that I had a drop in total income as I could no longer work a couple of nights on the *Sketch*.

Our children were a delight if you ignore the fact that when unsupervised they would flick mashed potato at each other with their forks in the breakfast room or hurl fallen, rotten apples at trains going past the end of the garden on a little branch line. However, when it came to taking them out to a smart restaurant or hotel they were perfect. No parents were ever prouder of their offspring.

Came a day when June could not get up. She had a severe attack of appendicitis. As the Croydon paramedics carried her out to the ambulance Beanie and Linnie carefully tucked up her blankets and gave her a kiss.

After the vehicle departed they plaintively cried: 'Who is going to get our tea...

who is going to get our dinner?' I managed but soon my mother was delighted to take over.

Thanks to an experienced ward sister the surgeon operated that night and peritonitis was averted. Came the time for a hospital visit.

The children were washed, shampooed, hair brushed and dressed to perfection by their grandmother before we set off. They would have passed inspection at the Maresfield guardroom.

I'll never forget the expressions on the three little faces, not to mention June's, as they ran into the ward. Everybody had a special hug. They lit up the ward. Everything had gone well, which was good, for a few days later we were due to go on the Broads for a boating holiday. June still had stitches in but that didn't stop us going and we had a great time. The Broads became a favourite holiday destination. The girls loved the wildlife occupying the banks, ducks and moorhen chicks swimming around the boat and the proliferation of birds.

Howard was to begin a lifelong love of fishing which demanded much more patience than I was able to produce. Ranworth Broad was a favourite overnight mooring where fresh rolls were delivered in a wheelbarrow early in the morning and roast chickens to order in the evening.

Of course everybody wanted a chance to steer the craft and Howard later learned to sail on the Broads with Trinity School. Soon, as in most families, we had a surfeit of skippers.

From the Broads we tried the Thames but although fun it never had quite the charm we experienced in Norfolk.

CHAPTER 8

Up the ladder at the Express

Stepping down from the editor's chair, albeit on a local weekly, to become a lowly sub-editor on the *Daily Express* was in many ways a shock. Once more I had to take orders rather than give them.

I was on three-month trial and really did not think I would make it. Looking back I realise I was trying too hard. As a newcomer I was not getting page leads or page one stories to handle. It was a nightmare three months that I somehow survived. I was switched to stone subbing – the last line of defence - working alongside compositors, re-writing busted headlines, trimming stories to fit and ensuring that pages went to press on time. The schedule was easy compared to what I had had to handle at the *Evening Standard.* Soon the Night Editor insisted that I was stone sub, particularly for Page 1 on big nights for the budget or general election issues.

As a coda to this Mike Christiansen, Managing Editor of the *Daily Mirror,* who had offered me a holiday relief job a few months earlier, approached me in the Press

Club one night and suggested I should call him. His father was the great Arthur Christiansen, a legend at the *Express* who had done more than any man to modernise the projection of news while maintaining its integrity.

Mike did not waste time. 'They tell me you are not happy at the *Express* and that you are the best stone sub in Fleet Street. How would you like to join the *Mirror*?'

I never discovered who 'they' were but Fleet Street was a village at the time. With a wife, four children, a home and a mother dependent on me it was some offer. It was just what my shattered confidence needed.

'Sorry Mike,' I said. 'It's a great offer but if I leave the *Express* after only a few months people will say I couldn't hack it.'

He understood. 'Well let's put it on ice and if you ever change your mind you know my number.'

Two nights later I went in to see the *Express* Managing Editor, Eric Raybould, a blunt Midlander. He had been in the Press Club and had seen Mike approach me. I began by saying I knew he saw Christiansen approach me in the Press Club a couple of nights ago.

'Oh that! It happens all the time.'

'Well not to me it doesn't and I've got a family to think about. What I want to know is; do you want me to stay here or not?'

'Well, you're pretty blunt and I'll be blunt with you. You had a dreadful start here but you're not the only one who has suffered that. I had a bad start when I joined the

Express. But we look on you as one of the guys of the future.'

'That's all I want to know Ray. I'll turn the offer down.'

With that I turned and walked out of his office. Two days later I got a note confirming my job on the *Express* and including a pay rise. Best of all I found myself sitting in as late copytaster, a task that offered me several chances to shine.

Fleet Street was a great place to be in the Sixties. For most people London was swinging: the Beatles, Carnaby Street fashion, mini skirts and the decade when Britain finally shook off the ravages of World War II and believed that in the words of Prime Minister Harold Macmillan that at long last they had never had it so good.

But there were problems beneath the surface. Serious commentators feared the Cuban missile crisis when Khrushchev and Kennedy stood eyeball to eyeball on the diplomatic stage while the world was threatened by the Cold War extending into a nuclear one and the extinction of mankind.

The revelations of Profumo led to one of the great Parliamentary scandals of modern times, the Congo was in turmoil, Vietnam was presenting itself as an insoluble problem and the Soviet Union invaded Czechoslovakia with impunity.

Kennedy and Martin Luther King fell to the assassins' bullets and Mao launched a cultural revolution in China while the West looked on helplessly.

At home Harold Wilson swept into power as Prime Minister of a Labour government that promised a white-hot technical revolution.

On the social side women had not made the breakthrough into leading roles in industry and management, the National Health Service struggled to contain cancer and heart problems and hyperinflation was a smudge on the distant horizon.

Cancer was a killer to be feared and three quarters of the male population still smoked. A cigarette was the accepted ice-breaker on a first meeting and a packet of 20 a day and often more was commonplace for the average man.

This surfeit of news fuelled the adrenalin, particularly on the *Express* which was enjoying its great days. One man who had believed in me to such an extent that he said he would quit if I was not offered a permanent job was Ted Dickinson, well regarded and a top table sub, who had been at the *Express* in Manchester and London for around five years. We became firm friends, played golf once a week with two other subs, Dan McDonald and Ronnie Higham, and he was a welcome visitor to Kenley where our children took to this gentle giant. He could also be stubborn, opinionated and very funny. I was so lucky that June really liked my friends: particularly

Jim, Max, Ted and Bill. In turn they thought she was special and never stopped pointing out that I was one of the luckiest men alive.

Every one of them could be described as people you really need in bad weather.

My early nemesis at the *Express* had been Morris Benet, chief sub-editor. He was known as 'the adjutant,' which he had been in WWII. He may have been in the infantry but he was a master of psychological warfare. I've seen him reduce grown men to near tears and he gave me a rough ride. Later he was to become one of my main supporters and I graduated to his chair when he moved up to Managing Editor. Long after he retired Ted and I used to lunch with him regularly which was always hilarious. We had to go to the Strand Palace because Morris had shares in it and got a 20 per cent discount!

Apart from my new status I took a part-time job locally editing *Golfing*, a monthly magazine. This occupied me four days a week 9 – 4 for which I received £15 a week and the use of a Sunbeam Rapier. The cash meant that Linnie and Beanie could attend a little prep school in Caterham called Eothen.

In those days I could drive straight from the *Golfing* office in Caterham to Fleet Street in half an hour to be on time for work at the *Express*.

Golfing was owned by a wealthy eccentric called Gordon Binns. If anybody ever had a schizophrenic personality it was him. One minute he could be all charm and the perfect host, the next he was an unreasonable four-letter man.

The second month I was there he sacked the advertisement manager and took off for Switzerland with a showgirl he had picked up from a London nightclub. I was left to sort out the pieces along with a charming woman who was his long-suffering secretary.

One person who became our best contributor was Peter Alliss. This was his first venture into journalism. He learned fast and did the groundwork enabling him to become a fine commentator on TV and a contributor to many magazines.

Fortunately Binns and I shared a passion not only for golf but also for cricket. I obtained tickets for the Oval Test against the West Indies and we had a good day out until he suddenly flew into a fury because, he said, I could always get served in a crowded bar and he couldn't. I lasted nearly a year before I handed him back the keys to his Sunbeam Rapier. He refused to sell me the car but on the day I left gave me a letter of thanks and a cheque for £350. Strange man.

I remember that car particularly because June and I used it to take the children to the first of several holidays in Cornwall, staying at Bennie's Farm on the Lizard. The Bennies also had two young children. Ours played happily with them and revelled in seeing the animals.

I also took Vivian Bennie, who was a year or two older than Howard, shark fishing off the Cornish coast.

The boys had a great time and the boat, owned by the famous Vinnicombe brothers never failed to return to port without a haul of mackerel and happy fishermen photographed alongside sharks they had caught. While we were fishing June had taken the girls to Kynance Cove and then for a cream tea.

Those farm holidays with the children were idyllic. I should mention that all our children had 'family' nicknames. Howard was Howardy. Linda was Linnie, Zena was Beanie and Sally was Kins. The latter came about because the older ones taught her to speak her name and address, in case she got lost. She could not say Jenkins but shortened it to Kins.

And Kins she has remained in the family. June was Mums and I was Dads. This worked until they became cool teenagers when their mother became June and I was John. After a few years teenage sophistication faded and we reverted to Mums and Dads.

Beanie was particularly patient with Kins who, as the youngest in a family often are, could be a little madam. She ran away from home once after being told by June to clean out her guinea pig. For provisions she took three of her favourite Cadbury's cream eggs but dropped one in a stream at the bottom of our paddock. We scattered north, south, east and west in our search and Lin found her and gave her a piggy back home. What a relief.

Not that the others were perfect. But they were just normal, happy, wonderful children: a great, loyal gang in any joint venture.

All the while I toiled away for Lord Beaverbrook. Roger Wood, who had been editor when I joined, left to be replaced by Bob Edwards, known throughout paperland as Piranha teeth. He was Beaverbrook's choice, much to the annoyance of Beaverbrook's Managing Director son Max and some members of the *Express* management team.

Edwards had several essential qualities as an editor: he was a good judge of events and people and took little notice of management. If he said jump it was not a subject for debate but first one to the ceiling. He had cut his teeth as a local reporter in Reading and then moved on to Sunday tabloids before editing the left wing *Tribune*. Like many good left wing mercenary journalists he saw nothing wrong in working for the Beaver.

By the time Edwards arrived in 1961 I was standing in on many nights as copytaster or late copytaster. This put me right under the eyes of the backbench. I should explain here that in newspaper terminology backbench equals the Parliamentary front bench. It's where the great and the good perform: Night Editor and his deputy, Managing Editor, Editor and anybody else with an exalted title and initial capital letters.

My luck really had changed, for every time I sat in as copytaster a big story broke. One concerned a three-line paragraph from Reuters to say a Greek liner, Lakonia, was on fire in the south Atlantic. So what? Not an unusual fate for Greek ships. It barely rated a paragraph in most papers and some actually spiked it of no interest. There was no follow up from Reuters for hours.

In a moment of financial madness I had booked the family on a Christmas cruise to the Canaries, had researched other cruises and knew the Lakonia had sailed a few days earlier from Southampton with 640 Brits aboard. Peter Johnson was Night Editor and I whipped around to tell him we had a major story.

What followed was a classic example of how the *Express* newsdesk, foreign desk and picture desk all swept into action. Within half an hour we had a lead story on Page 1 complete with a stock picture of the ship for the main edition of the night...all from a two-line snap.

Nobody else could catch up. More than that, we had chartered an aircraft to fly over the burning ship the following day with photographers who recorded the calamity. More than a hundred passengers lost their lives.

I was off the following night but when I returned I found a little brown envelope in my pigeon hole. It was a note of congratulations and thanks from Bob plus a 33 per cent increase in pay.

On nights when I was late stop it meant that when the backbench had gone home or to the Press Club about 12.30a.m. I was left in charge of the paper. If there was anything of note I could re-plate the front page to include later news.

I did it so often that Johnson was irritated that his beautifully designed front page was re-modelled by me. 'If something breaks you can put it there,' he tried telling me, indicating a minor position.

'Really? Supposing the Queen is shot?' He gave up.

I could change the front page up to about a quarter to four in the morning. After that it was too late.

Came the night of a South American football disaster when more than 300 people died as police lost control of spectators in Lima, Peru, when the national team were playing Argentina. Police had let dogs loose among the crowd which panicked. It was one hell of a story and I was going to run it as a major single column top on Page One, when Ted Dickinson, who had been to the Press Club walked in on his way home to pick up a paper and asked if I had had a quiet night.

I showed him the agency snaps.

'It's a lead,' he said.

'I know,' but I haven't got the time to do it.'

He took off his jacket and said, 'I'll sub it. You do the layout and the re-jigs.' And we did: the only paper to lead on it that night.

On one occasion I had a mild reproof from the editor. Ian Macleod, a leading Tory MP, spoke in the Commons saying that he often disagreed with the *Express* but on this occasion the paper was right. He added that as it was so late (around 3.30a.m.) Max Aitken would never know.

I squeezed that story in with minutes to spare and by the time the House rose at 6a.m. Parliament Square was ringed with *Express* vans carrying placards saying Macleod Backs Express on Trade. MPs could pick up the paper on their way home. Ron Turner, the night circulation manager, was a live operator and took up with alacrity any of my suggestions.

Apparently a few MPs had telephoned Max Aitken to say what a great bit of enterprise, and he rang Bob Edwards at home. 'You and I have had our differences Edwards but congratulations on this morning's paper.' And put the phone down. Bob didn't know what he was talking about. When I went in the following night he met me in the corridor.

'Well done John, but you might let me know what you are going to put in my paper.'

'Sorry Bob, if I had stopped to phone you, we wouldn't have made it before lift off.'

'You could have phoned me afterwards,' he said quietly, giving me his famous Piranha teeth smile. I made a mental note.

It wasn't long before I was sitting in the chief sub's chair with Ted at my side as copytaster. His judgement was superb. It was like having Jack Charlton at centre half in England's World Cup winning team. Nothing got past him.

Added to that, sat in front of me was the best team of sub-editors in Fleet Street.

I remember Ted coming down to Kenley where the children thought the world of him. Linnie, all of five or six asked him if he had a wife.

'No,' said Ted, 'but will you marry me?' She thought seriously, asked him if he had any saucepans and he replied not many. So she turned him down.

Years later Lin was shifting as a reporter on the *Express* when Ted was Managing Editor.

'Hi Lin,' he said as he passed her in the corridor on her first night. 'Hi Ted,' she replied.

One of the staff reporters gasped. 'How do you know Lin Jenkins?'

'Oh, I asked her to marry me once and she turned me down,' Ted said without breaking stride. I was delighted to be his best man when he married Sheena in Edinburgh, daughter of the *Edinburgh Evening News* Editor Max McAuslane.

All the time I was reporting a Saturday match for the *Sunday Express* and on one occasion at Upton Park, the old West Ham ground, spotted a familiar figure walking towards me along a corridor at half time. He had that look which translates as: 'I know you but I can't remember from where.'

'John Jenkins, Mr Brown, from Jimmy Dutfield's adoption meeting in Blandford a few years ago.'

'Good god, what are you doing here?'

114

'I'm covering the game for the *Sunday Express*. What are you doing here?'

'I'm a West Ham supporter... have been all my life. Where can we get a drink?'

At that moment Reg Pratt, chairman of WHFC and chairman of East Ham Conservative Association walked down the corridor.

I made the introductions and Reg took him into the directors' lounge for a drink. I left the deputy leader of the Labour Party and the local Tory chairman happily discussing the merits of Billy Wright and Bobby Moore. They remained great friends.

We feared, but didn't realise how quickly, that when Beaverbrook died in June 1964 the light would go out for Express Newspapers. His son Max, a brilliant sportsman and wartime RAF pilot, DSO, DFC, succeeded him but died a year later. Edwards was replaced by Derek Marks, a sound political editor but lacking other essential requirements.

I had met Max a couple of times. The first was the time-honoured ritual of a tap on the shoulder and a secretary to tell you that you were invited to a fifth floor lunch on Tuesday 12.30 for 1p.m. This was a hint that you might be destined for higher things. Could you talk the talk and did you eat peas with your knife?

The lunch was fascinating. Max treated us as if we were a crack squadron going to take out some vital target in the Ruhr.

At the time Prime Minister Harold Wilson had a super chief of staff called Marcia Falkender. She seemed so vital to the running of No10 Downing Street that there were rumours she was Wilson's mistress.

'What's the truth of this?' demanded Max. 'Is Wilson having it off with her?'

Marks sighed. 'There's no bloody truth in that at all. She is having an affair with Walter Terry, Political Editor of the *Daily Mail*. That's why the *Mail* is getting the best political leaks.'

Poor old Derek. Good that he was, he couldn't compete with pillow talk.

'Well can we use that?' said Max.

'No we can't,' said Marks wisely.

'Well write it anyway and put it in the safe. We might be able to use it one day,' said Max. Everything else after that was a bit of an anti-climax but I often wondered what happened to the contents of that safe.

In the background the NUJ was pushing for a formal pension scheme for journalists on the *Express* group. Unfortunately it was difficult to find anybody still alive who had retired. We tracked down Charlie Roper who had been Foreign copytaster and in retirement for two years. We asked him what pension he was getting?

'Don't go stirring that up,' he begged, 'I'm still on full pay.'

Typical of the Beaverbrook management attitude was a decision following the death of Bob Thrale, a good sub editor, who succumbed to a heart attack. His wages stopped after one month and a deputation went to speak to Tommy Blackburn, the general manager about his wife Judy and children. The father of the chapel opened up about principles and Blackburn cut him short. 'Don't talk to me about principles, talk to me about money. What do you want?'

The Father of the Chapel thought quickly. 'Full pay for a year so Judy can complete her examinations as a librarian and a pension thereafter considering she has two children.'

'Done,' was the reply.

On one occasion I was in the editor's office when the picture editor brought in some superb candle-lit photographs of Britt Ekland, sat up in bed with her new born baby. The pictures had been taken by her husband, Peter Sellers, who was a gifted photographer as well as a fine actor. Bob asked me for my opinion. 'Great stuff for a photonews spread.'

The picture editor said that Sellers wanted £500 for the pictures. Edwards agreed but the picture editor hesitated knowing that Bob had been told by management that his limit to buy any picture was £250. The Editor merely shrugged away the objection: '£250 for the picture and £250 for the caption,' he suggested.

Express parties, particularly on Maundy Thursdays were great fun and always produced a fund of stories. In those days nobody published on Good Friday which seemed to be the only time we were all free and could get together.

One of my more bizarre adventures at the Express concerned the purchase of a horse. It came about 3a.m. one quiet morning when Ivor Key, the late duty reporter, Mike Brown, Paris correspondent over for a meeting with the editor, and another reporter whose name I have forgotten, thought it would be a good idea to buy a racehorse. Ivor, who rode out work for a trainer John Benstead at Epsom, knew where there was a horse for sale at a reasonable price and we decided to share the cost: 25% each. When it came to signing cheques only Mike and I signed up and the trainer Wibberley agreed to keep a third. Colours were registered at Weatherbys and we entered the sport of kings with the resources of vassals.

On a Sunday we journeyed to Wantage where Wibberley had his stables and met Methane, an eight-year-old chestnut. According to my small girls he was lovely: but to them anything on four legs was wonderful. June wondered what kind of state I was in when I agreed to the deal. Methane, himself, did not look much of an athlete.

We watched him run in a hurdle race at Warwick that was hock deep in mud. It was part of his fitness training. He finished exhausted, much like I would have after a two mile cross-country run. Wibberley said: 'Wait till you see him next time.'

Next time he looked fabulous: shiny of coat and bright of eye. Wow! Wibberley had him entered for a race at Wye in Sussex and we were going 'to have it off.'

At my suggestion we booked Josh Gifford, one of the finest jockeys of his generation, for the ride. So to Wye. I was recovering from jaundice at the time and not at my best. June did her best to look like the Queen as we talked to Wibberley in the paddock. I persuaded her that she did not need to wave to the crowd.

Wibberley left us for a moment and came back looking worried. 'What do you know about Ocaretto?' He asked Josh. 'Dunno, he's been off the track for a long time.' I had had the biggest bet of my life, several hundred pounds, and wondered whether I should have a £50 saver on Ocaretto. No, I thought, enough was enough. Wrong decision. Despite a fabulous ride by Josh, Ocaretto at 10 -1 beat Methane by half a length, catching him on the run-in after Josh had led over the last hurdle. A week later Methane won a seller at Hereford, and although we bid up to £800 somebody topped us and he departed from our ownership. The girls never forgave me. I breathed a sigh of relief: our venture into the sport of kings had not been a total loss.

Back at work the *Express* had become a different paper. The maverick attitudes and fun had gone out of the job and Marks was a reluctant editor. In fact he told us on his appointment that *nobody in his right mind would want the job.* Bankers joined the board that had hitherto comprised men who worked their way up in editorial, production, advertising and circulation departments.

Before the financial men moved in there was a postscript to the traditional *Express* ways. Sydney Smith, an excellent foreign correspondent, was on one of his periodic visits to London. The visit followed the usual pattern: lunch with the Foreign Editor, lunch with the Editor, back slapping and hand shaking around the newsroom and foreign desk. There was also the small matter of expenses.

Sydney sat at a desk, much like I had seen George Whiting do and sent page after page up to accounts. Down came a numbers man.

'It says here, Sydney, that you spent the equivalent of nearly £100 on a camel?'

'Sure did. The only way to get up Kilimanjaro to the air crash site. He pulled out a diary and quoted a date. 'Couldn't get a car up there.'

'I see,' said the abacus man and retired, only to pause and return. 'So now the *Express* owns a camel?'

'Damn,' said Sydney, 'I forgot, it died on us and cost me £40 to get it buried.' He added the sum to the sheet in the hands of the accountant.

Marketing, design and financial control apparatchiks moved in and editorial influence slipped down the ladder. After five years, it was time for me to move on. David English, one of the best journalists of his generation and Foreign Editor at the time, thought likewise and proved to be the saviour of the *Daily Mail* and *Sketch*. He could, and should have been the saviour of the *Daily Express*.

Deadlines all my Life

CHAPTER 9

Joining the Daily Torygraph

If I were to move on, where could I go? The *Mirror* was still the biggest selling paper, the *Mail* clearly needed a shake up and so did the *Daily Telegraph* after Roy Thomson, another Canadian entrepreneur, had bought the *Times*. The bounder was actually planning to put news on the front page of the Thunderer, instead of classified advertising. Mike Taylor, a friend and chief sub of the *Mirror* invited me to a *Mirror* party where I met the then current Night Editor, Larry Lamb. Good journalist that he was, and later architect of Rupert Murdoch's *Sun* success, I doubted if he and I could ever get on so I ruled out the *Mirror*.

Acting on information received, as they say in the police handbook, I wrote to Roy (later Lord) Thomson, Lord Rothermere (Mail) and Michael Berry (later Lord Hartwell). Replies from the first two said Thomson and Rothermere were out of the country but I would be contacted later. Michael Berry asked me to fix an appointment with his Managing Editor, Roy Pawley.

The interview went well and although I did not get the figure I asked for, I got a promise that if I was still there after three months my demands would be met.

Pawley was a strange man, rather like Captain Mainwaring in Dad's Army. In fact his voice and pompous delivery were similar.

'I was on Eisenhower's staff, y'know,' he confided. Later he was named as an MI6 contact who instructed *Telegraph* foreign correspondents to give British intelligence all the help they could. Nothing new there. Several senior editorial men had worked for intelligence during the war.

My farewell party from the *Express* ran over two nights. It was held at Aunty's in Dorset Rise. Cannot say that I remember much about it, so it must have been good. Later, June was to tell me that I was wrong to have left the *Express* and she may well have been right, I had more fun there than at the *Telegraph*.

The *Telegraph* planned that as an initiation into its ways I would do a month's home subbing, a month's foreign subbing, then stand in as revise sub editor, followed by stints as deputy chief sub editor and chief sub. On my first night the tanker Torrey Canyon ran aground off Cornwall: a huge pollution risk. Copy poured in like an avalanche and it would have been easy to be overwhelmed. Despite the fact that I had not actually subbed a major story for two years (having been a

124

member of the Back Bench) the story read well and an exacting initiation was successfully negotiated.

But in quick succession the chief sub editor died from a heart attack and the Night Editor retired. I turned up one day to do my stint as revise sub which began at 5p.m.only to be told:

'We've been trying to reach you all day. Can you take over as chief sub?' Normally that job began at 3p.m. so I started two hours behind. The *Telegraph* had a daft system whereby not only did the two copytasters (foreign and home) read everything, the same copy was delivered to the Night Editor, his deputy and the chief sub.

My home copytaster was Norman Palmer, a man of excellent judgement and great experience. I decided the only way we were going to get the first edition away on time was to use the *Express* way. 'Have you read all this Norman?'

'Yep.'

'Good. I dropped my copy into a nearby bin, picked up the news schedule and the dummy, which contained blank pages for news with advertising spaces marked, and said: 'Give me a choice of three stories to lead page three.' That's how, despite the late start, the edition went away on time.

Norman knew what the *Telegraph* needed and marked my card when I was not sure. We were to become friends and I often went to Langley Park in Kent to play golf with him. He was undervalued and should have risen much higher in the *Telegraph* ranks. Somewhere along the line he had crossed the Night Editor, Peter Eastwood, as had another stalwart, John Ralph.

Eastwood, (despite a unique gift for making enemies) held the place together. Perhaps, because he had to wait far too long to become Night Editor and Managing Editor, and see lesser men promoted, he was inwardly embittered. Harry Winslade was a live wire as Night News Editor and the newsroom boasted an outstanding team of reporters and specialist writers. They also had a very go-ahead City Editor in Ken Fleet and the best Parliamentary correspondent in Sir Harry Boyne. Perhaps I misread Pawley if he was the man responsible for recruitment.

But the quality on the subs' table was poor. In time I persuaded Eastwood to move on or get rid of the worst while excellent, experienced successors in Mike Harman, Roger Evans, Peter Durrant and Clive Barrow were recruited. They transformed the place and the whole standard improved. The subterfuge I had to use to get these people paid a competitive Fleet Street rate was astonishing. While the purse strings for my sub-editors were difficult to loosen, the cash poured into the *Telegraph* magazine was nothing short of profligate. I learned that it had cost more than £3000 to send a photographer and two models to the Sahara for a fashion shoot – a feature that could have been equally well shot at Sandbanks. However, one magazine feature cost them only buttons.

To this day I do not know who put me up to be featured in the *Daily Telegraph* magazine. Despite being one of its more vocal critics I had never met John Anstey, the Editor. However, one of their feature writers was assigned to describe how I put together the front page of the newspaper and a photographer shot three reels of 35mm film for two pictures, one of which occupies the front of this book. The ribbing I got from all and sundry went on for a week. Only one person never mentioned it: Peter Eastwood. Was he the mischief maker?

Strange to say not a week went by without a row with Eastwood who, despite being a talented journalist, was something of a bully.

He also lost a good chief sub in Tom Eyton who was given an insultingly low salary increase when promoted. For some time Tom had been thinking of quitting and that made up his mind. He left and with his wife Audrey launched *Slimming* magazine. After a precarious start it proved a fantastic success and the Eytons sold it for a reputed £3million. They deserved every penny.

A newcomer to the subs' room was a son of Lord Hartwell, Adrian Berry. Quite charming and inoffensive, he was known from his days with the reporters as Adrian Berri Berri and was described as our science correspondent. I was handling Page One that night and Eastwood said I should give the lead story to him. He repeated the instruction as a look of incredulity passed across my face. I did but then had to re-write the introduction myself. After the main edition at 12.15a.m. Eastwood used to arrange for a few bottles of brown ale to be delivered to the Managing Editor's office. The only newspaper in Fleet Street to have a licensed canteen was the *Telegraph*. This scruffy bar was sarcastically known as the Starlight Room. These lukewarm beers were delivered by a messenger in a dirty white jacket.

On this particular night, however, with Berri Berri joining us, the messenger appeared not only in a smart, clean white jacket but also with a tray of smoked salmon sandwiches. 'My word, these are good,' said Berri Berri. This was too much for Rod Junor who was standing in as foreign copytaster that night.

'Did you order these, John? Are we going to get this kind of service every night?'

I couldn't stop laughing at Eastwood's discomfiture and that wrote the start of the end to Roddy's career at the *Telegraph*.

On several occasions I broke the golden rule by editing copy myself. One occasion concerned a division in the House that occurred as we were going to Press. A messenger brought the result of the vote to me which was important enough for me to rewrite a sentence in the introduction to the lead story and delay the moment of going to Press by a couple of minutes.

The compositor handling Page One locked up the chase with the new type, gave me a blanket pull of the front page and slid it into the foundry for moulding into a cylinder. Strolling back to my chair, known for obvious reasons as 'under the clock,' I read the proof and realised to my horror I had written the name of the Chancellor of the Exchequer as Roy Jenkins when in fact it was James Callaghan. I raced back to the foundry and for the first and only time in my life shouted, ' hold the front page.' The edition went away 15 minutes late, but at least it was accurate. If that had gone on the streets I'm sure that even at the *Telegraph* it would have been a hanging offence.

As for the *Telegraph* management, with one or two notable exceptions, it was indecisive and incompetent. In fact the whole show was strange. The scale of their incompetence was shown up several years after I had left. How it could get into such an awful financial mess when Hartwell and Maurice Green were graduates of the *Financial Times* I could never fathom.

The editor, Maurice Green, was a clubbable figure who looked after the leader page and oversaw features. He dined at Number 10 and reported direct to the editor-in-chief, Lord Hartwell. It was the Managing Editor who had the responsibility for news, sport and production. He too, in this strange dichotomy, reported direct to Hartwell.

They all went home at 7p.m. and the Night Editor was in charge. That suited me just fine when I progressed to the chair. The editor would pop in for a five-minute chat before he went home to ensure that I was carrying stories that referred to his leaders.

Unlike many national papers the *Telegraph* did not have a lawyer on the premises. Instead I had a hot line to Peter Carter Ruck, the best libel lawyer in London. If I had a doubt about a story I could always ring him for advice. The conversation, around midnight, would go like this:

'Hi Peter, John here. I've got this story about Emil Savundra...'

'Well, you wouldn't ring me up John unless it was libellous, would you? But he hasn't got any reputation so he won't sue you. Go ahead if you like.'

In Hartwell's favour, if his journalists were right he would back them all the way up to the House of Lords and did so.

One event that exemplified the difference between the *Express* and the *Telegraph* came when I received the customary tap on the shoulder and was invited to lunch on the fifth floor. So far, same drill.

On entering the fifth floor suite, which Hartwell occupied, I was met by the butler. Sherry or cocktail, Sir? What's the cocktail I asked, only for him to repeat the previous mantra. With Max Aitken you helped yourself.

Then in to lunch. Each person had a small pad and pencil in his place, no doubt, to note down great thoughts. It was like a dreary country house with the conversation neither interesting nor enlightening. Certainly no great thoughts.

At the end of lunch port was passed around. If there's one drink I cannot enjoy it is port. (It triggers gout). I noticed that Hartwell preferred scotch and had a bottle of Johnnie Walker black label at his elbow.

I asked him if I could have a scotch. 'Certainly,' he replied and sent the bottle down with the butler. I took the bottle away from the butler (with a slight struggle) and poured a generous measure. Hartwell was almost inarticulate at lunch and did not seem to enjoy company at all. That was misleading as I discovered one night at the height of trouble with the printers.

The unions were trying to dictate editorial policy and a few days earlier the *Observer* had been forced to print a front page with a blank space instead of a picture because of their censorship. Three nights later, just before the main edition was to go away at 12.15a.m. the night production manager rang me to say the printers were refusing to run the paper because of a trade union story by Blake Baker.

The *Telegraph* had its faults but it was very strict in not mixing opinion with facts in news stories. Blake was the best industrial correspondent in the business. His reporting was straight down the middle.

I rang Eastwood who told me to ring Hartwell. The next exchanges could have been straight out of the second act of a Brian Rix farce. A French maid answered the phone at the Hartwell residence which was a stone's throw away from the Commons in Cowley Street and a ten-minute drive from Fleet Street.

'Can I speak to Lord Hartwell, please, John Jenkins here.'

'Ee ees not 'ere.'

'Well, where is he?'

'Ee ees asleep.'

'Well wake him up.'

'I cannot wake him up.'

'Look, this is the Night Editor of the *Daily Telegraph*. You must wake him.'

Did this girl not know that night editors sit at the right hand of God and have to be obeyed?

Eventually Hartwell came to the phone, asked me to get the printers' union people up to his office and said he was on his way.

He arrived in a coat over his pyjamas, was articulate, determined and courteous.

I drafted a few words that the printers accepted, inserted two paragraphs into Blake's story and the edition was saved. I decided to take a page proof up to Hartwell but the lights were out and he had gone back to Cowley Street, no doubt where the maid would make him a cocoa. Very different to the man I had met at that stilted lunch. I subsequently learned the maid was not French but Portuguese. Further inquiries I felt could prove indelicate.

Within reason I could do what I liked with the paper. I was the first to put a boxing picture on the front – Cooper losing to Bugner in a disgraceful decision – racing when the French stewards stood down Lester Piggott at Longchamp and one of Nick Garland's excellent political cartoons of Wilson and Roy Jenkins dressed as chefs cooking the books above a caption that said: 'If you don't like the heat stay out of the kitchen.' I still have the original in my study.

On one night I threw out £2,000 of advertising. One of our photographers, a former Yugoslav partisan called Djukanovich, but known to us all as Chunky, was on his way back from Windsor Great Park where Prince Charles had been playing polo. Suddenly a BEA Trident which had just taken off from Heathrow flew over his car and crashed in a field in Staines, killing 112 passengers and six crew. Chunky was off and running almost before the heads and other body parts had stopped rolling in the grass.

The picture editor was first to warn me before we got an agency message.

Five minutes earlier I had been searching for a lead story among a load of tosh and suddenly the decision was handed to me on a plate.

Chunky's pictures were fantastic but many were too graphic to use. Not at all the sort of thing to see over your toast and marmalade. That took care of the front and I dropped a huge advert from page three to make way for more pictures. It was an airline advertisement and I knew airlines never advertised if they could avoid it after an air crash. Then I got a reporter, Brian Silk, to interview Chunky on what he had seen. Tough guy that he was, Chunky was severely shaken. We had the best coverage in Fleet Street.

I rang the advertisement director to tell him I had dropped the advert. He was about to explode when I gave him the reason and he ended up thanking me.

For some time I had been moonlighting for BOAC producing their weekly staff newspaper with a crack team of mercenaries from Fleet Street: Ted Dickinson, Bert Morgan, Mac Keane, Andy Carson, and Dan MacDonald.

Hence it had the best staff newspaper in Britain. It was also self-funding, for Leslie Sellers, star night editor of the *Daily Mail* and author of *The Simple Subs Book*, Mac Macklin, a senior PR for BOAC and I worked out that we could devote four of the 12 pages to classified advertising which an agency near St Paul's never failed to fill. This paid for the 20,000 run and my team. Win, win all round.

Leslie disappeared from the scene and my team took their fees in a combination of cash and trade exchange for flights. Hence I knew something about airlines and how they worked. When BEA and BOAC merged into British Airways it was even bigger and better. The new editor was Rodney Calver and he was great to work with.

This meant that when June told me she was expecting Sally we booked a quick flight to Malta and a holiday in the sun to give her a break. We had a marvellous week.

Thanks to my British Airways connection I was also invited to be a guinea pig passenger on their first Boeing 747 flight to New York. When our airline decided to buy this massive new generation aircraft from Boeing there was great dismay in Parliament.

Pity the same concern was not shown in the future development of Concorde or the TSR2. In the event the criticism was muffled when agreement was reached that some of the 747s would be equipped with Rolls-Royce engines instead of Pratt and Whitneys.

To New York as a guest of British Airways was a treat. We stayed in a hotel on Lexington Avenue, dined with the New York Chamber of Commerce in the Empire State Building, trawled Broadway and Greenwich Village and travelled up and down Hudson and East Rivers seeing wonderful sights. I don't think I went to bed for three nights.

Along with David Henshall, a former colleague from the *Evening Standard*, we called in unannounced at a precinct police station. We were both fans of Ed McBain's stories featuring the 87th precinct. After early

135

suspicion the cops welcomed us like brothers. 'Hey, if you're British you'll want a cup of tea.'

With great ceremony huge mugs of the worst tasting tea I have ever known were produced which we drank assuring our hosts it was terrific. However, I must say that wherever we had coffee: in the Empire State building restaurant or on the boat taking us around Staten Island, it was excellent. To this day I have the Artie Shaw record I bought in a shop off Broadway at 2a.m. and I still cannot make up my mind whether Goodman or Shaw was best on clarinet.

We had hired a taxi driven by a huge Bermudan who had served in the British merchant navy during the war. Around four in the morning we began to walk back to the Lexington, when he pulled up alongside. 'Don't go walking in New York at this time of night,' he advised. We insisted we were all right and then he said: 'Look, if you haven't got the fare hop in. It's all right.'

We still declined his offer but he tailed us all the way back to Broadway ensuring we were safe.

*   *   *   *

Although parts of the *Telegraph* were far removed from Fleet Street caricatures, it still had its share of role models for *Private Eye's* Lunchtime O'Booze, not to mention Teatime O'Booze and Dinnertime O'Booze.

One member of the features staff and his lady used to inhabit the King and Keys next door, from roughly

1.30p.m.to 3.30.p.m.and later from 7p.m. to closing time. However, they could not stay friends for that long and at chucking out time would resort to fisticuffs. By then both had difficulty in standing. As luck would have it, in the few yards between the *Telegraph* and the K & K there was a huge old-fashioned double post box with individual openings. One would curl a right arm into the slot as a steadying mechanism while flailing away with left hooks. The other would push her left arm through the other slot and retaliate with right crosses. Although many blows were hurled few hit their mark none did any damage and colleagues would bribe a taxi driver to take them home.

At one time the *Telegraph* sponsored the intrepid explorer Colonel John Blashford-Snell, a man determined to go where no man had been before. A star reporter was assigned to cover one of his hazardous forays into a frozen polar wasteland. Clearly the brave reporter needed some suitable kit for the journey and requested £400 in advance expenses for thermals, ski gloves and suitable boots. The chit was duly signed by Pawley in mid-afternoon; the cash drawn and by 11p.m. the newsroom had drunk the lot. How our man in the frozen north did not die from exposure has never been revealed.

On another occasion I needed to talk to Colin Welch, the deputy editor and found him cowering on his knees in the corner of the editor's office as his mistress hurled everything she could lay hands on at him, all the time shouting: 'You've got to pay to educate your bastard.' The girl had a point of view. Colin had initiated the Peter Simple column. He also rode a motor bike to work and could do amazing impersonations of Ian Paisley. Why he was Deputy Editor I could never fathom.

I still worked for the *Sunday Express* and began covering football and cricket matches for them as well as acting as late-stop sub editor.

The combination of outside income gave me more than enough confidence to deal with any efforts by Eastwood to upset me. If I disagreed with his view he used to fall back on...'well the owner wants us to...'

'Does he?' I would reply. 'Then let's go up and see him right now.' Eastwood always backed down.

Despite his total lack of people skills he was an exceptional journalist and amazingly well read. When he died, a short while after retiring, the *Guardian* published a bitchy obituary on him to mark the occasion. That says more about the *Guardian* than it did about Peter.

Union intervention was becoming more and more of a problem. After one stoppage we found that all the 'pots' had gone cold. It was the days of hot metal type and the pots contained a mixture of lead, antimony and tin that would only operate at about 50 degrees. From cold they took an hour to reach optimum temperature. When the Honourable Hugh Lawson, a species of night production manager, turned up to give Eastwood the news, Peter recalled his days in the army in the Far East. 'When we had that problem we used Chinese coolies with blow lamps to get started early,' he said.

The Honourable Hugh looked at him with disdain. 'Terrible dearth of Chinese coolies in Fleet Street, Peter,' he replied.

After seven years it was obvious to me that even if my final, probable position was to be Managing Editor it was not going to be enough. And I could faintly hear the bells of hell going tingalingaling for newspapers. If Tom Eyton could make a fortune from a magazine, surely I could.

Deadlines all my Life

CHAPTER 10

We move out to the country

We enjoyed a comfortable lifestyle. June and I adored our children, mother was comfortable, we had two cars, a caravan and a lovely home. My job in Fleet Street was as safe as any in that precarious profession, so why mess things up?

The *Telegraph* was no longer a challenge. I could have run the whole shooting match and if Hartwell had any sense he should have offered to make me editor of the newly-launched *Sunday Telegraph*. It needed, if not me, then somebody like me to challenge the *Sunday Times*. It would also have needed a Beaverbrook to take that kind of risk.

I was going to have to start up on my own: but what with? I was no Mr Micawber and had not saved a sixpence from each £ earned. There was, however, equity in the house. It would have been easy to realise some of that with a second mortgage. Instead, we sold Kenley for £32k and bought Horseshoe Cottage for £27k, moving to the countryside in East Grinstead with four acres of land

and various outbuildings. It was a huge gamble but we looked upon it as an adventure.

On the plus side it included a cosy, self-contained granny annexe comprising a kitchen, bathroom, sitting room and bedroom for my mother, a bedroom for each of the children and stacks of space for the menagerie the children acquired by stealth.

The little copse we inherited was full of rubbish so that was cleared. One of the outbuildings was so decrepit it was demolished and burnt. Another one was re-roofed and made waterproof. Decorations were done. The bathroom panelled, attic rooms made habitable for children and a fitted kitchen installed. Paddock fencing was replaced and reinforced as necessary, a loose box built and a hay store constructed. We were on the edge of Ashdown Forest, near excellent fishing in a local reservoir and surrounded by nothing but fields and trees. Next door, in Horseshoe Farm was Kenneth Quick, an outstanding horseman who owned a dozen or so greys which presented a stunning sight in his paddocks when they were turned out. He ran a riding school and also supplied horses for films where he was frequently a rider. My girls thought they were in heaven.

On the downside it stretched my journey to London and Howard's to Croydon by half an hour while Linnie and Beanie transferred to Sackville, a local comprehensive. Kins began at an infants' school called

Fonthill Lodge. On the downside, instead of a five-minute walk to a station it was a 10-minute drive.

East Grinstead was a lively little town with some history and many amenities.

I did not think much of Sackville Comprehensive School, but to be fair, from there Linnie and six or seven of her contemporaries gained places at Russell Group universities, including two to Oxford.

All the family took it in their stride and loved it but I have always had a soft spot for Kenley. We had put so much of our life into that house. Nevertheless our Horseshoe Cottage ran it close. Howard, who had been on a study holiday in Vienna to learn German, brought back an American student, Bill, who had a few days to kill before heading on to the States. He was a terrific help in filling skips with rubbish.

Various others pitched up once we were settled: sometimes for lunch, sometimes a day or two, sometimes for weeks and June welcomed them all: Veg, Nicky, Karen, Mark I, Mark 2, Mark 3, Chris, Lance, Martin, Nigel, etc. I'm sure I have missed out some names. Although we lived at the bottom of a lane that was a cul de sac it was incredible how many boys called in because they were 'just passing.' It was a fine place to bring up a family: our dream.

It was the start of what I think was our Camelot era, but it did not come without a struggle.

I was on the hunt to buy two magazines. They had to be cheap and capable of development. The idea was to put them under one roof and by sharing services such as rent, phones and other overheads turn them into profit.

My accountant, Norman Bloom, introduced me to the Manager of Barclays in Cavendish Square and he liked the premise and agreed to match my £5,000 with a similar amount. The hunt was on. I found *Greyhound Magazine* which was bombed out and for sale and another one in different ownership called *London's Pubs,* geared towards tourists. Not the most sophisticated titles but they fitted my criteria. I agreed a price for *Greyhound Magazine* and the owners of the other title. The proprietor of *Greyhound,* who could be described as a likeable rogue, stuck to his word. The other party, all white shirt cuffs and public school drawls, tried to gazump me on the price 24 hours before completion. I walked away from them.

I took the problem back to John Mellors at Barclays. 'Oh dear,' he said, 'then the deal is off.'

'Wait a minute, supposing I continue my job at the *Telegraph* and work part-time on *Greyhound* until I find another title.'

'Could you do that?'

'Yes.'

'OK then,' he replied. We were in business. All I had to do was work 16 hours a day.

Buying *Greyhound Magazine* from Norman Bowles had been a triumph of stamina and guile. He was an estate agent, property developer and wheeler-dealer on many fronts. Later I learned that he had begun life as a coalman. His contacts were extraordinary, ranging from council officers in Windsor to highly placed officers at Scotland Yard. They were all on his payroll in cash or kind.

We had a day-long meeting in Hayes where his office was based which included an excellent lunch at a hotel on the edge of Heathrow. He wanted £10k for the magazine. I offered him £5k. 'What do I want £5k for? I've got £5k in my pocket.' Later, we were joined by a commander from Scotland Yard.

Norman then asked me what I was doing that evening and would I like to go greyhound racing at Wembley Stadium? Sure. Something told me to stick with him.

He rang his girl friend Jenny and asked her to book a table at Wembley and meet us with the Roller in Wembley car park. Sure enough, as we pulled into the car park in a little Morris 1100 from his estate agency office, there was Jenny, all dolled up, driving a green Rolls-Royce registration NB 100. Kisses all round. In the restaurant was a table for about eight. As far as I could tell nobody paid for anything except Norman although I insisted on buying a bottle of wine.

'You don't have to do that,' said the commander, who was acting as runner for Norman, placing bets with the bookies, 'Norman picks up the tab.'

At the end of the evening Norman asked me how I was going to get home. I had not taken a car. 'If I can get back to London I can get a train, I suppose.'

He had a better idea. 'Take the Morris 1100 and return it to Scotland Yard's front desk when you go to work the following day. If anybody stops you, tell them to ring this number,' which he scribbled on a piece of paper.

I drove home and returned the car before I went to work at the *Telegraph*. Nothing happened for a few days. Then he rang. Would my wife and I like to be his guests at the famous names charity ball at Grosvenor House, Park Lane?

Sure. Delighted. On the table were directors from West Ham Football Club and Wimbledon Greyhound Stadium, the Medical Officer for Health for Windsor and a different commander from Scotland Yard. All with their partners.

As ever, Norman was a generous host and joined in the charity auction to raise money for a coach for disabled children.

During the evening he danced with June. 'I like your husband,' he told her.

'So do I.'

'I'd like to help him but he'd probably tell me to fuck off, wouldn't he!'

'Yes, he probably would,' she agreed, not turning a hair.

Two days later we did the deal for £5k.

The first issue was a disaster. The second much better and every issue seemed to improve. Then I was whipped into hospital at 45 minutes notice suffering from a severe attack of haemorrhoids.

Any fellow sufferer will know the pain and embarrassment this nonsense causes.

From my hospital bed I asked June to phone Bert Morgan and Mac Keane, tell them the problem and ask if they could come to the rescue. Despite the fact that they were both my friends they had never met until 4p.m. at my attic office in Dorset Rise just off Fleet Street.

Bert, chief city sub-editor on the *Telegraph* knew all about dog racing as well as enjoying an encyclopaedic grasp of Stock Exchange matters, and Mac, a rising star on features at the *Daily Mail,* was a wizard at layout. Between them they brought out the next issue. Neither would take payment but some years later I gave Mac the basis of a wine collection from El Vino's and provided Bert with a selection of Waterford glass. Friends like that are very rare.

This publishing business was a steep learning curve. Out went one of the joint editors who was averse to work, out went a dodgy bookkeeper and an unsatisfactory ad manager. Neil Martin stayed and was invaluable as editor while Les Dilbey, an assistant racing manager from Catford Stadium, had all the greyhound contacts and learned to be a good ad manager. The wife of a friend took over as bookkeeper on a temporary basis and June ran the subscription side. I often stayed up all night editing copy and doing the page layouts ready for the printer to pick up at nine the following morning.

Even the children helped. Every so often we would take the magazine around tracks where there was a ready sale. Linnie and Beanie wore *Greyhound Magazine* T-shirts with aplomb and sold plenty of copies. Even Kins modelled for the front cover with a greyhound classic winner.

On Greyhound Derby night at the White City I had permission to park my caravan in the stadium and with eight sellers, all students, we sold 2,000 copies. Soon the title had stopped losing money and turned in a useful profit.

One of my best gimmicks was a monthly lunch in the top room in the Cheshire Cheese in Fleet Street, two doors away from the *Telegraph*. They still have Dr Johnson's table available in the downstairs restaurant. I subscribed to the good doctor's favourite maxim: 'Nobody but a blockhead writes except for money.'

I used to invite eight greyhound track managers who were told they had to bring a story. Neil and Les sat at one end of the table, I sat at the other and thanks to the stories the event took care of itself. The menu was always the same: smoked salmon, the famous Cheshire Cheese steak and kidney pie as main course, cheese and biscuits and the house claret. We never booked fewer than six pages of advertising and I only wish I could remember some of the stories: ribald and far-fetched as some of them were. One involved an Irish entry for our Greyhound Derby. The owners refused to kennel the dog with any British trainer but smuggled him into the Savoy hotel and took him out through the kitchen for a walk along the embankment for exercise.

Special guests were Len Went, PR for Wembley, Charles Chandler from Walthamstow, Bill Holmes from White City and guests from Harringay, Catford, Wimbledon and Hackney. We even persuaded Southend and Brighton to put in an occasional appearance.

Posting out the subscription copies was an example of cottage industry: Horseshoe Cottage. We had topped the 1,000 mark that meant we could qualify for a special discounted postage rate providing we delivered the copies in bundles to the local sorting office according to their postcodes.

With help from Karen and Nicky and others we whipped through the lot and I delivered them direct to East Grinstead sorting office. A few spare copies for the post office staff plus a crate of beer at Christmas ensured they weren't shoved aside but given priority.

I also realised that the key to the magazine was not the gambling side but breeding and the volume of stud dog advertising. This is what really helped us to turn the corner. We introduced a useful spin-off book called *The Greyhound Magazine Guide to Stud Dogs*, edited by Alan Lennox.

Then came a real crisis. Not just for us but the country. Ted Heath, one of the worst Conservative Prime Ministers in our history, took on the miners and lost. This plunged Britain into a fuel crisis and an enforced three-day week for industry. Only essential businesses were allowed to operate normally. Greyhound racing took place mostly under floodlights in the evening and was not essential. The phones began to ring with stadium managers cancelling their advertising. In desperation I took the phones off the hook and later said we had gone to Press, it was too late to cancel. As different areas had different periods when power was available we took electric typewriters home and worked in relays with the London office.

Ever resourceful, some tracks switched to afternoon racing and the ban was soon lifted. Crisis management was something I learned on the run. You would need to be Damon Runyon to do justice to many of the stories surrounding greyhound racing. Ireland was the big centre for breeding dogs and I went over a several times.

On one occasion I went to Shelbourne Park in Dublin for the Irish Greyhound 600, a classic race. The place was heaving and a waterfall of money was changing hands with the local bookies. A popular British owner, Freddie Worrell, had a runner which won and his group celebrated in style at the track and then repaired to the Shelbourne hotel, (or was it the Gresham?) where the party continued. Champagne all round. Freddie had had, in the local parlance, a right touch. Around 3 a.m. an anxious waiter appeared at Freddie's side.

'Mr Worrell, sir, I'm afraid we've only got Dom Perignon champagne left at £45 a bottle.'

'What,' said Freddie in mock alarm, 'you mean to say we have not been drinking the best?'

Great fun but I still had to find another title to seal my escape from Fleet Street.

Deadlines all my Life

CHAPTER 11

Recruiting a great team

Many titles were examined: many discarded. Then a suggestion came from two unlikely colleagues, Norman Palmer and John Ralph. They knew about my plans to quit the *Telegraph*. Did I know there was a growing interest in retirement and there was a magazine in Croydon devoted to the subject? *Pre Retirement Magazine*, I discovered, was run by a little known educational charity called the Pre Retirement Association (PRA). The magazine was funded by a philanthropist called Michael Pilch.

Michael had made a handsome profit when the insurance broker Noble Lowndes was taken over by a merchant bank. He had also retained his directorship.

I first contacted the PRA and they referred me to Michael. I met him in his elegant office in a new, high-rise block in Croydon. He wore a smart, dark blue suit, white shirt and Balliol tie. I had worked in Vienna with a Balliol man and had seen at first hand why they had a reputation for adopting an air of 'effortless superiority.'

On his desk was a notice saying: No Smoking. He was poles apart from Norman Bowles. Negotiations were going to be on a vastly different level. Michael wore his status more lightly than my friend in Vienna. He listened as I outlined my publishing plan. I had not mentioned *Greyhound Magazine* but concentrated more on my role at the *Telegraph* that I considered more his cup of mint tea.

'I accept that you have an impressive background in national newspapers but what do you know about magazines?'

I took a gamble and told him about *Greyhound Magazine* and how I had turned it from loss to profit in 14 months. 'How interesting,' he enthused, 'when I was at Oxford some of us used to buy greyhounds from Ireland and race them at local flapping tracks.'

He then told me about a tale surrounding a fellow undergrad at Oxford who had dreamt about a horse race and a winner. His friends all piled into a car and spent a day at Newmarket where the horse won. Thereafter they tried re-creating the exact process in terms of food, drink and bedtime to get him to dream another winner. 'All to no avail,' chuckled Michael. The ice was broken.

I felt that I had just backed a 25-1 winner. The deal was done in principle but he had turned the contract over to his Family Trust lawyer and it was no simple matter. He was in every sense a practical philanthropist. His Trust supported me with a Debenture and an agreement that I would pay the PRA a royalty of one penny a copy sold above 11,000, the current circulation of the magazine.

I faced a number of problems. I needed a partner as I could not bowl at both ends and keep wicket. I needed a secretary as my existing one, Jay Patmore, had decided to retire. I needed an ad manager...the list seemed endless.

I needed the PRA onside and spent time with them researching the area of retirement planning. They were hugely supportive, particularly Fred Kemp, the secretary/director, Bill Bruce who succeeded him and Dr Beric Wright, the chairman, who was also BUPA's chief medical officer. Like Michael Pilch, Beric was also a first class writer.

The more I studied the scene the more convinced I was that I knew the man to join me. He was John Kemp, social services correspondent at the *Telegraph* and a rising star.

My luck was in. He agreed to join for the same salary as he was getting at the newspaper but he wanted a car. Any sort of car. It was essential as his wife used one to get to work as a teacher and he needed one to get to the station. I agreed at once and went home to give June the good news. The bad news was that I had agreed to give him her car, a little Morris 1100. How she put up with me I'll never know.

JK and I had our leaving party at the Cheshire Cheese where he was presented with an antique village pump for his garden and I received a pair of binoculars and a set of Mozart's works recorded by the Berlin Philharmonic. I seem to remember that John was wrestling on the floor in the Cheshire Cheese sawdust as I left but of that I cannot be sure. He complained that he had to carry the pump all the way to Liverpool Street Station because no cab would agree to pick him up.

I'm glad to say the Cheshire Cheese is still thriving but many of Fleet Street's pubs have gone, been re-named or gentrified into gastro pubs or perhaps ghastly pubs. A favourite for the *Express* was Aunty's at the bottom of Dorset Rise behind Reuters. In the 19th century Fleet Street was alive with brothels, known locally as aunties. They had all disappeared (as far as I know) by the time it became the home of newspapers.

The Old Bell, the Punch, the Albion, El Vino's, the Tipperary and Poppins all had their followers while a little further away the *Daily Mail* colonised the White Swan, re-naming it the Mucky Duck, and the *Mirror* occupied the White Hart and re-named it The Stab, short for stab in the back. And the Old Press Club off Dorset Rise had its dedicated supporters. Before it moved to the chrome and plush surrounds of the Press Centre in Shoe Lane the Press Club was redolent of memories and faded glory, cartoons by Spy and talk of exclusives and unbeatable poker hands. Twice a year it featured in my diary in red ink. One event was the children's party which Linnie and Beanie attended. This was held for children aged from five to eleven or so. Beanie was only four when she first went and when an announcement was made for anybody under five to step forward she stayed schtum. They were not going to catch her out. Nurses from Barts Hospital were drafted in to look after the children who departed with a huge bag of prezzies each. The other unmissable date was the Derby lunch. One memorable guest was Suzy Volterra, certainly the most glamorous of French racehorse owners. She was introduced by Peter O'Sullevan, the *Express* and BBC racing correspondent who knew everybody who mattered in racing on both sides of the Channel and the Irish Sea. Suzy epitomized French glamour and style.

As my daughter Lin is fond of telling me: Dad, you wouldn't like the newspaper business now. Like most fathers I have from time to time embarrassed my children. One night I met Linnie in the Mucky Duck for a drink after she had finished her shift as a reporter on the *Mail*. Another reporter from the *Mail* joined us and after a few moments said: 'You don't remember me, do you Mr Jenkins? I used to work for you in Stratford. It wasn't for very long. You said I would never make a reporter in 100 years.'

'Oh dear. That sounds like me but I'm glad I was proved wrong. What would you like to drink?'

After he left I apologised to Linnie. 'Is he any good?'

'No, he's rubbish.' I felt a little better but not much.

A few months later I called in at the *Telegraph* late one afternoon and bumped into the editor, Bill Deedes, who was travelling up in the lift. He had made a witty speech at my leaving do. 'Good heavens, what are you doing back here,' he asked. 'We always look upon you and John Kemp in the same way that fellow prisoners looked at the escapees from Colditz.'

* * * *

Details of how we produced the first few issues of *Choice* are hazy but one crucial gap was solved by an old friend, Rodney Calver, from British Airways days. I was desperate for a good secretary and he said he knew somebody who was perfect. He was absolutely right. Anthea Ware became an integral, vital part of the organisation and has stayed a friend to this day. She was much more than a secretary. She was probably the most intelligent person working with me and a great sounding board for ideas and people. She was also totally loyal.

Money was going out at a frightening rate. Little was coming in.

It was time to see John Mellors at Barclays Bank to discuss in detail an additional   facility to finance the operation. A couple of days later he said no. Unknown to me, a Debenture, which Michael's Trust had taken out, ranked in front of any loan the bank would make.

'If the trust will waive their claim, I can lend you the money. By the way, can I have a copy of *Greyhound*

Magazine's accounts.' We duly arranged a meeting to follow up his requests.

Worse was to follow. No accounts were forthcoming and I called at Norman Bloom's office but he had disappeared. I later discovered my friendly accountant had had a mid-life crisis, deserted his business and gone to America to open a travel agency. I had no audited accounts, only a management set.

'Oh dear,' said John Mellors. 'Can you repay your existing loan this week?' An official letter demanding repayment followed this polite request.

After several unsuccessful attempts to raise more money I was in despair and was due at Brighton greyhound track one evening. Somehow I couldn't face sharing the hospitality in the directors' box, where I was always welcome, and stood alone on the sparsely occupied terraces.

Suddenly a massive hand rested on my shoulder. 'Hello John, what's your problem?' Clearly problems were evident from my expression. The speaker was one of my best *Greyhound* advertisers, an ex Welsh cruiserweight boxer who had built up a thriving business selling surplus powdered milk, meat and other products from Ireland to greyhound racing kennels. As there were many kennels in the country, mostly with more than 200 greyhounds each, he was doing well.

I told him *Greyhound* was fine but *Choice* was still haemorrhaging money. 'Go and see my bank, Allied

Irish Bank in Croydon.' So I did and met Dermot Moloughney, an engaging, straight-talking rugby wing threequarter who moved with all the speed and agility you could expect from a specialist in that position. Among the questions fired at me were two I remember: '*Greyhound Magazine* company is making money and the *Choice* company isn't yet?'

'Right. But it's improving. See management accounts.' Audited accounts for Greyhound, supplied by Casson Beckman, were good.

'And your wife supports you in this venture?'

'100 per cent.'

'OK. What we'll do is lend you the money secured on the *Greyhound Magazine* Company. Unofficially, what you do with it is your business.'

That was the start of another great connection that eventually led me to advising AIB on Public Relations in Britain. They went from two branches in Britain to 30 in three years and Gerry O'Mahoney, their UK general manager, and Dermot became my allies.

By now I had a properly constituted board of directors for *Choice*. It included Michael Pilch, Dr Wright, Fred Kemp, (Manager of the Pre Retirement Association); John Kemp, June and Advertisement Director Tony Weller. It would be difficult to overestimate the roles they played in the success of the enterprise. Apart from contacts and suggestions their mere presence meant that I had to accept the discipline of accounts on time and accurate periodic reports. Beric and Michael were no mere ciphers. The recruitment of Tony Weller was the result of another introduction, this time from Mac Keane, then a key figure at the *Daily Mail*. He introduced me to Tony who was number three in the *Mail* advertisement set up. We had lunch a couple of times and he made some helpful suggestions. I said to him: 'You know you are going to join me some time, Tony, why not now?'

'You couldn't afford me, John?'

'Why not take out a pencil and paper this weekend, write out your own contract and show it to me on Monday? Then we'll see if I can afford you.'

It looked ok to me, we shook hands and he joined the team as a vital piece in the jigsaw. For two years Tony took much more out of the company, in salary and commission, than either JK or I did, but long term it was a great move. The only mistake he made was to miss taking out a £2000 share option that would have made him a lot of money.

Before Tony arrived on the scene it looked as if we were going to Press without an advertisement on the back cover. I thought a building society would look good and approached the Halifax advertising agent Brunnings. I got the usual brush off given to a new publication.

'Sorry old boy all the budget is allocated.'

'Surely you have a contingency budget?'

'Yes, but that's with the client and you'd have to go to Halifax to talk about that. Ha ha.'

I gave the Halifax a call and arranged to meet the marketing director. Standing aloof from rows and rows of Coronation Street type houses stood a building that looked as if it should be the American Embassy in Brazil. All copper glass with pink stone at the top of steps that would have graced St Paul's or St Peter's in Rome. The interior was quieter than a cathedral with thick carpet and open plan at which sat attentive staff working away. I met the marketing director who received me warmly and listened quietly to my pitch. I doubt at that stage if I was very professional but at least I came across as believing fervently in my magazine. The crux of my argument was that my readers had plenty of disposable income and would be an excellent source for boosting the Halifax coffers.

The marketing director smiled and said: 'We've just spent £30,000 on a survey to prove what you have just been telling me. Would you like a copy?'

That alone made the trip worthwhile.

He followed up: 'What are you doing for an introductory offer?'

'We're doing three back covers for the price of four.'

'You don't mean that, do you?'

' Yes I do.'

Then I gulped. 'No, sorry, I mean four back covers for the price of three.'

He laughed. 'OK, put us down for four at the price of three.' Halifax stayed with us for ten years, not only as an advertiser. We produced a series of booklets for them.

I walked back down the hill to the station. Any fool can sell advertising, I thought. But of course any fool can't.

John Kemp came to the company's rescue at one sticky point by taking out a second mortgage on his home that gave him a substantial shareholding. It paid off handsomely for him and he deserved every penny.

Another plus were our accountants, Casson Beckman and in particular Peter Ohrenstein, a senior partner who was virtually a non-executive director, and audit manager Peter Hill. They had been introduced by our lawyer, Laurence Marks who had his office in nearby Bulstrode Street.

A strange phone call led to an even stranger lunch. A headhunter telephoned me to say he had to fill a senior position for a journalist and could I spare a little time to meet him. No I couldn't, I was far too busy. He replied: 'Surely you can stop for lunch.' We duly met for lunch and he told me the job was chief executive of Reuters. He was friendly and asked how I would frame the job specification. When I had finished he told me I had described the requirements exactly and he was authorised to offer me the job. If he had come a year earlier I would have accepted. I explained it was impossible as I had just set up my own business.

'Couldn't I get somebody else to run that for me?' A couple of years later, maybe, but certainly not then. The only person I told was June.

I wondered who had tipped him off about me. Lord Hartwell? Doubtful. Possibly the chief executive of PA/Reuter, George Cromarty Bloom. His son, who like many youngsters, had not settled to anything joined my team of reporters in Stratford, and had proved himself a capable operator. So George had invited me to lunch several times at his dining room in the Reuters' building to thank me. He had also followed my career into Fleet Street. It remains a puzzle. I recommended Ken Fleet, the City Editor of the *Telegraph* who was quite brilliant and responsible in part for the huge upsurge in advertising in the Saturday home finance pages. Ken, however, had his eye on the editorship of the *Telegraph.*

We were outgrowing our little office in Dorset Rise and were on the lookout for new premises when Barbara Spiers and her husband, great supporters of the PRA, suggested I approached the old GLC (Great London Council). We did and moved into a suite of offices in Covent Garden, the third floor of Bedford Chambers, at a rent of £4 a square foot and rent free for six months in return for refitting the cloakrooms and decorating the place. It was a steal.

Covent Garden was magical. We had views over the piazza, street entertainers, super pubs and wonderful restaurants. The staff loved it. London's Apple HQ now occupies our old offices – I guess they are paying a touch more than £4 a square foot.

Anthea and Sue, JK's secretary, were anxious to see our new home and I took them there one evening and settled who was going to work where. The only snag came from the telephone company. We would be without phones for three weeks. *Of course, they could work overtime on Saturday (£125 in cash)* but they would need a dust free, near sterile room to house the exchange kit. It was Friday afternoon, and the offices had been unoccupied for two years.

'OK,' I said. You can begin tomorrow morning at 8a.m. The room will be ready.'

I rang June. At 6p.m. she appeared with cleaning kit, paint, brushes, lino and two helpers: Linnie and Beanie. By 9.30p.m. we were done and the little room was immaculate and dust free. The phones were duly installed, I handed over the readies and we didn't lose a day's selling time.

All my children had part-time jobs. Howard worked at a garage on the petrol pumps, before the days of self-service, Linnie worked in a greengrocer's and then a bar in East Grinstead, while Beanie put in a shift at a local boutique. Lin and Howard invented the everlasting pint. Howard bought one and then as two thirds of it disappeared the glass took itself across the bar and was mysteriously refilled without any more money changing hands.

We recruited other good people, notably John Birch a gifted Art Director and great team player, and his deputy, Marlon, a huge Rastafarian from St Lucia.

We sublet some of the offices to the Institute of Journalists. Then Bill Tadd, the News Editor of the *Telegraph*, who had fallen foul of Eastwood, joined us on an ad hoc basis. Bill was a great asset, friend of John Kemp's with an acute editorial mind and the ability to make the unworkable work. In his wake came his partner Hillary. Like most creative people she was at times impossible, but she more than made up for this with positive contributions. Almost single-handedly she persuaded fashion houses to use mature models instead of those with stick insect figures to portray fashion for mature women – our *Choice* readers.

Hillary had been secretary to Lady Georgina Coleridge, the autocratic editor for *Homes and Gardens* for 25 years and a director of IPC magazine group. They had a love/hate relationship. JK, who had a marvellous way of dealing with contributors, got the best out of both of them. We had lots of happy lunches at her home in Kensington and her husband Arthur, a director of *Readers' Digest*, a big untidy chap, never objected to being called My Lord when abroad with Georgina. Her title was hereditary. Arthur invented abridged books for *Readers' Digest* which were a huge success.

In fact Lady G, as we called her affectionately, virtually adopted John and I, referring to us as her lovely boys, and warning us not to take any notice of Hillary's sillier ideas. She also tipped us off that **IPC** were thinking of launching against us. When Lady G wrote for us we didn't pay her cash we gave her a subscription to *Raceform.* She was friends with Dorothy Laird, a biographer, who used to go racing with the Queen Mum, which is how we got an exclusive feature for the Queen Mother's 80th birthday.

By now we were publishing a stable of magazines and booklets. Not all were successful. I had a visit from a couple of schoolmaster entrepreneurs who alerted me to the huge profits made from school textbooks. This was their proposition. The GCSE syllabus for English papers was critically short of contemporary poetry. They were in position to recommend four poets to fill the gap. However, their collections had to have been published in print runs of at least 2000 each with the capability of satisfying a much greater demand if taken up.

The poets were George Macbeth, Lucien Stryk, Susan Musgrave and Galway Kinnell. Nobody could doubt the quality of their work and we paid each author £500 as an initial tranche.

All went well and the books looked as good as the excellent contents. Then one of our entrepreneurs went on holiday to New York, met an American girl, married her and returned to live in New Zealand never to be heard from again. His colleague resigned from teaching to become successful as a writer and did not return calls or answer letters.

We had 8,000 poetry books with a cover price of £2 each which JK remaindered for sixpence a copy. You win some, you lose some.

At 20 when the world was my Oyster...

June on her 16th birthday

June with Sally
watching Punch
and Judy in
Rome

An early shot of
us returning
from a camping
holiday in
Scotland

Posh frocks and DJs celebrating an award for Choice Magazine.
Carol Kemp, JJ, Brenda Lowe, JK, June and Bill Lowe.

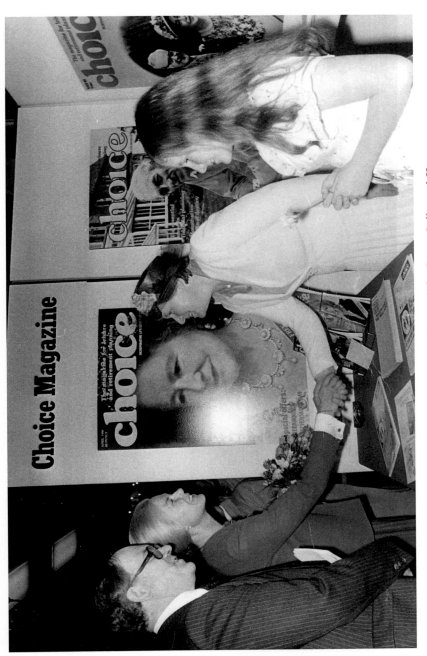

The Duchess of Kent has come to see the show. Welcomed by June, Sally and JJ

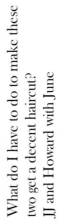

What do I have to do to make these
two get a decent haircut?
JJ and Howard with June

SANTA MARIA

GOLF & COUNTRY CLUB

Marbella Costa del Sol

My castle in Spain

JJ and June on her 50th birthday

"IF YOU DON'T LIKE THE HEAT – STAY OUT OF THE KITCHEN!"

June with Sally

The mums: June's and mine

Winner of the Bulbury
Grandmother's Cup
- and her inspiration

Grandmothers Cup. The one trophy June was determined to win

June and Zena

CHAPTER 12

Mrs Thatcher threatens to sue

In 1976 we could not afford a December Christmas party for staff but by mid 1977 we could. So we had one in June, complete with turkey and Christmas pudding in a restaurant underneath the arches at the bottom of Ludgate Hill. The arches and the railway bridge across the bottom of Ludgate Hill are now long gone.

Roughly at the same time I did a deal to hire five Datsun Cherry cars for the price of four. In addition, Tony had a mid-size saloon, JK had a Ford estate and John Birch a sporty sort of Vauxhall. All this did wonders for morale.

We also began to embrace new printing technology and did our own typesetting. This meant we could set five magazines for the price of two and we had two good operators working six-hour shifts each day.

We had also embraced the business of producing magazines for various hotel groups, Ranks, Grand Metropolitan, British Rail and Corals. Very upmarket and very glossy. About this time JK and John Birch nearly collapsed when I returned from lunch and said I had bought another couple of magazines. They feared I had acquired two more titles not just gone shopping at the newsagent.

JK and I also produced a one-off tabloid newspaper celebrating the final of a Granada Bingo national competition. Our mini PR consultancy was growing all on its own with Spillers Dog Food (sponsors of the Greyhound Derby), the National Association of Pension Funds, (NAPF), Halifax Building Society and Allied Irish Banks as the main contributors. *Choice* spin offs included booklets on health and financial planning (updated after each budget) for those approaching the end of their working life plus a retirement briefing file.

Our influence and the list of blue chip companies were expanding fast. We numbered Allied Breweries, Unilever, Fords, Legal & General, Shell, Barclays and the BBC among our clients.

Choice subscriptions were growing well thanks in part to our links with the National Association of Pension Funds and a yearly stand at the Institute of Personnel Management Conference in Harrogate. Peter Edwards joined as subscription manager and did a good job. So did Anthea because we soon learned that a man in a suit on a stand was off putting for many delegates whereas Anthea, wearing a Laura Ashley dress, was welcoming. At the Harrogate conference I spun my old *Greyhound* trick. We invited a dozen big firms to lunch: six of our clients and six prospects. Peter sat at one end of the table and I sat at the other making sure the glasses were topped up. We let our clients do the selling.

At the end of each Harrogate conference we would celebrate with dinner at Box Tree Cottage restaurant in Ilkley which each year was among the top four restaurants in the UK. It was a long way from my days on the *Standard* when lunch, if any, was egg on toast in Gamages.

We were moving so fast we were in grave danger of overtrading. It often takes place when companies expand their operations too quickly and accept work that requires greater resources (usually cash or people) than it has available.

Also, I had not taken a holiday for two years which was unfair on the family. Christmas came and I felt that by adding a few days to the traditional break I could well take time off. I had however, left it far too late and everywhere seemed booked solid. ' Never mind,' I said to JK, 'I'll forget about it.'

That brought a swift reply. 'You need a holiday,' he retorted, adding, 'and we need a holiday from you.'

He certainly had a gift for words. 'Seeing you put it so nicely I'll try again.'

In desperation I rang friends, including my old racing partner Mike Brown in the *Daily Express* office Paris. 'Any suggestions? Anywhere, must be four bedrooms, sun or snow I don't care.'

He suggested Andorra. Where was that? Oh, that Andorra!

That's how we came to spend Christmas skiing in Andorra after driving through France. Imagine a winter sports holiday in Aspen Colorado, or Kitzbuehl or Verbier. The height of luxury and sophisticated après ski entertainment.

Now imagine the exact opposite, basic in the extreme. Après ski entertainment was watching the Spanish and French argue over which country's TV programmes to watch.

Despite that we enjoyed it. The family were together and Kins was a menace on her little plastic toboggan as she hurtled fearlessly down the nursery ski slopes. I hope the staff enjoyed my absence.

Financial management was still something I was learning and thanks to Beric I had joined the Institute of Directors and had attended their excellent courses on finance for non-financial directors and computerisation. It was one thing to identify the problem quite another to solve it.

One solution was to sell *Greyhound Magazine*. It looked as if I had done this to the rump of Amalgamated Press that had been split up, re-named and re-formed after an IPC takeover. I had met several of their directors and one of their editors who would be responsible for it. At a lunch in the traditional home of such deals, the

Savoy Grill, we shook hands on a price of £60,000 and I strolled away enjoying a cigar. Quite the tycoon.

The euphoria lasted three days before they rang up to say the deal was off. No explanation, and no apology, or at least one that I can remember. I was in a state of shock. That was when JK - unasked - came to the rescue with funds from a second mortgage on his home. He also assumed a much wider editorial role as I was taken up more and more with management responsibilities. Staff relations were easy as we slipped effortlessly into good cop, bad cop roles. No prizes for guessing who was the bad one.

Credit control was another bugbear. London advertising agencies would often delay payment for up to three months claiming they had not had voucher copies or invoices. This was rubbish but what could a small publisher do against such giants? A new neighbour changed my attitude. He came in for a drink one night and asked how things were going.

'On paper fine but cashflow is a problem. Agencies were paying me in an average of 45 days: some were spinning it out to 90. I was paying my printer within 30 days and of course the staff wages.'

'Look upon it as theft John. They have had the service and if they don't pay you on time, as agreed, treat it as such.' I underwent an epiphany moment.

Invoices and voucher copies were then hand delivered to the worst culprits and had to be signed for. Statements

173

were banged out with warnings in red and my ace in the hole was to ring up and ask, 'If you don't have the funds should we approach your client direct and ask for payment?'

We even sued the mighty McCann Erickson, second largest agency in the world, for a mere £212 and received a furious phone call to say we would never get another advert booking from them. 'Could you repeat that please, I didn't quite catch it.'

They did. 'Fine, I said, I now have that on tape and will send it to your client.'

I refused to accept their cheque from a motorcycle messenger they sent round.

'Pay it into court with costs,' I advised. I did not have to approach their client.

Talking of suing people brings me to Margaret Thatcher.

We always put a personality on the front of the magazine who had something pertinent to say about retirement. Bob MacDougall, a BBC announcer for example, was furious when he had to retire when he could have continued reading the news. Another with something to say was Margaret Hilda Thatcher.

John Kemp interviewed her and reported that she thought it safer to stockpile a tin of corned beef for retirement rather than save a £1 as a hedge against inflation. This was a crack against Jim Callaghan who, as Chancellor, had run the country close to hyperinflation.

It was a good quote and Thatcher enthused on how her mother had taken such a prudent step during the war when rationing was introduced. JK didn't tell her that his family came from Grantham in Lincolnshire and were registered with her father's grocer's shop. It was not generally known at the time she was a grocer's daughter. Neither did JK report it.

Sitting at home on a Sunday morning I read that Margaret Thatcher was likely to run for Prime Minister. Our magazine was due out four days later.

JK immediately released our interview to the BBC and the national Press with a copy of the magazine. Many papers lifted our story wholesale without attribution but some and the BBC gave us credit. It would have been impossible to buy that kind of publicity. But the 'blessed Margaret,' or 'Attila the Hen' as wits like St John Stevas and Clement Freud named her, was not amused as the Heathites seized on this as an example of why she was an unsuitable candidate for Prime Minister. Conversely, many women among our readers applauded her views.

Thatcher's advisers were not convinced. They tried to deny the story and threatened us with legal action. The lady herself also wrote to me claiming the article was inaccurate. She also demanded herself that we should not run part two of the article in our next issue. One of her advisers, John Gorst, threatened me with legal action. I asked him on what grounds. He blustered on. I said we would be delighted if Thatcher sued us. We could do with some more publicity. As for accuracy, we had John's tapes of the interview which were securely locked away: not in the office. We didn't want a 'Watergate raid.'

I also wrote to Mrs Thatcher pointing out that our mailbag was showing 5 - 1 in her favour. We never brought up the fact that John's parents had been registered with her father for their groceries. We were saving that for court, if necessary.

Strange to say, I consider her one of the best Prime Ministers in the last 100 years. My other three are: Lloyd George, Churchill and Attlee. They all achieved what they said they would do. The Welsh Wizard changed the course of the First World War, Churchill's achievements are without parallel and Attlee improved the standard of living for British people despite the fact that after World War II the nation was bankrupt. As for Thatcher, she promised to end the anarchy fostered by trade unions and did so. None of them, despite their great qualities, were without faults.

Thanks to good contacts with Shell, who supported the PRA and Choice, we were able to use the Shell theatre on the south bank for the association's annual general meeting. This was a huge benefit for it enabled me to invite Shirley Williams, then at her peak as a Labour politician, to be our guest speaker. I remember introducing her and saying it was time Britain had a woman as a Prime Minister and she could be the first. At least I was half right. She received a standing ovation for a brilliant speech focused on retirement. I felt the Labour party was mad to lose her, David Owen, Roy Jenkins and Bill Rodgers. They were true guardians of the Labour party soul and founding the Social Democrats was never going to survive financially.

Our first big breakthrough for *Choice* came from Allied Breweries where Maurice Oldfield was pension fund director. His chairman was the ebullient, maverick

Keith Showering. They decided to give every pensioner a subscription to *Choice*. That was 7,000 copies in one hit. Then in 1979 they took over Joe Lyons and added another 5,000 to the order.

Maurice proved a great ally in the pre-retirement and pension fields and when he became chairman of the National Association of Pension Funds we were appointed PR advisers. I was out and about so much, speaking here and there and waving the flag for *Choice* that on one occasion I had to ring Anthea from Waterloo and ask, where am I supposed to be going today? I had discovered that once you put your name on the door you had to become your own top salesman.

Doug Hosegood of Unilever was another great supporter. He wanted an easy-to-read newspaper to explain what this massive fund did for 90,000 pensioners. Could we help? Indeed we could and did.

At one rather dreary session at an NAPF conference in Brighton Doug and I played hookey and went to Wheelers for a long lunch with Colin Flower, Pension

Fund manager for Bowaters. He placed an order for his people approaching retirement. I asked him if I could buy my paper from his company but sadly he told me they could not compete with the Scandinavians and had just closed a paper mill in Scotland at Fort William. He did, however, put me in touch with two of his old colleagues who worked for Lamco, the agency that imported paper from Finland.

They were based in the Haymarket and regarded me rather curiously. Compared with their other customers, many national newspapers using tons of newsprint every day, I was a minnow.

'You say you were at the *Daily Telegraph?*'

'Yes.'

Did you know the managing director Mr H.M. Stephens?'

'Of course I knew his majesty,' I replied using his Fleet Street nickname.

'Would you mind if we rang him?'

'Go ahead.'

The response was clearly favourable and ended with HM, a former Battle of Britain fighter pilot, saying, 'John Kemp and John Jenkins were two of our best men. Anything you can do to help them we will very much appreciate.'

Lamco looked after us superbly and that deal was worth £25,000 a year on what we saved on printing paper. More than that, they put their technical experts at our disposal and warned us to order in advance if a dock strike was looming.

As the influence and circulation of *Choice* grew so did the reputation of the Pre Retirement Association. Barbara Spiers wanted to start a London branch and asked me to be chairman. I was already deputy chairman of the national body.

The pennies per copy royalty we were paying each month added nicely to the PRA coffers, clearing its debts and helping in other ways.

Publishing is a minefield for the unwary. Printers, distributors, wholesalers and retailers seldom lose. Publishers do. Of 20 magazine titles launched in our first three years, only two survived, *Car* magazine and *Choice*. Our first print run was 70,000 and I discovered some years later that 35,000 never left the distributor's warehouse despite his promises. I was more fortunate with printers and quickly learned how to frame a contract that worked in our favour not theirs.

One of our printers turned out to be Nuffield Press, founded by motor magnate Lord Nuffield, formerly William (Bill) Morris, to print parts manuals and magazines for the Morris Owner, the M.G Owner and his other marques.

This works was at Cowley, Oxfordshire, home of the motor factory where Nuffield's original office was kept – rather like a shrine - just as the day he left it for the last time. Being something of a motoring nut and a former

179

beneficiary of the Nuffield Centres for servicemen, I was keen to see it.

The floor was covered in a remnant of the wine coloured carpet used in the Wolseley 12. An ancient intercom phone rather like those used in first World War trenches was on the desk, an engineer's drawing board stood ready for ideas, and on a cabinet was an array of proprietary medicines of the day, including Owbridges lung tonic, Milk of Magnesia and aspirin.

Stories surrounding him say much about the man. On the 21st anniversary of the company the workforce subscribed sixpence each to buy him a car off the production line. He never drove another vehicle for the rest of his life.

His foreman, also called Bill, had strong Socialist principles and he frequently argued with his boss. To put an end to their differences Nuffield said to him on one occasion, 'You really believe in all this equality, don't you Bill?'

'Yes guvnor.'

'And I'm worth about £8million.'

'If you say so.'

'Well, there are 48 million people in this country which works out about half a crown each. Here's yours. Now shut up.'

They remained firm friends.

Small cars have always been the salvation of the British motor industry and the Morris Minor was no exception. Lord Nuffield looked at the prototype and the drawings just before it was due to go into construction. 'Cut it down the middle and make it four inches wider,' he ordered. His engineers gasped.

'We're all tooled up ready to go, guvnor.'

The great man insisted. Make it four inches wider. And that's why the Morris Minor outsold the Austin A35 and became a classic of the British motor scene. So if you find an old one in a barn somewhere today – buy it.

I found that I could get on with printers, not just Nuffield Press, and we had great service from all of them and seldom changed. This meant for a relatively calm life.

Then **IPC** managing director Ron Chilton came knocking at our door, chequebook in hand.

Deadlines all my Life

CHAPTER 13

The threat from American bucks

I took immediately to Ron Chilton. He liked horse racing, so did I, and his brother John led a trad jazz group, John Chilton and the Feet Warmers, where the incomparable George Melly was occasionally the singer. I liked jazz, too. Ron opened the batting by saying he admired our magazine, was impressed by what we had achieved and would we like to sell?

'Everything I've got is for sale – at a price – except possibly my wife and don't offer me too much for her.' Sometimes my humour was in very poor taste. A king's ransom wouldn't have bought June.

The price he dangled was £60,000 (for the magazine, not June). Later, as we became friends he said he realised at once that I was not even going to sell him my desk for that.

Then came the sting in the tail: quietly.

'Of course, we could launch against you.'

'I know, and you have a budget of £250,000. But because we are small and dynamic we can make every one of our £s do five times as much work as your £.' It was a bluff but they withdrew and we remained on good terms. Ron was no fool and guessed that Lady G, one of his directors, had marked my card.

Then another suitor came a-knocking at the door: Synergistic Associates Incorporated from the United States, where retirement planning was big business.

Once more there was an offer and a similar threat, made by their company president, Walter Slawski. He and some buddies from SAI had defected from the American Association of Retired Persons to spread the gospel of retirement planning according to Wall Street to the world.

Slawski began with the idea of taking over the PRA which he described as having achieved very little. Beric replied that we seemed to have achieved enough to bring him 3,000 miles to knock on our door. Beric then gave him a short lesson on the British approach to state pensions and occupational pensions and weighed in with some pertinent facts on the NHS. He underlined the essential differences between the British and American way of life. Even Slawski could see he was no match for Beric.

What SAI needed was a reputation for probity and a campaign to sell a life policy to Britons over the age of 50 – without the necessity of having a medical examination. At the time it was unique although now many British insurers offer it and use greybeards like Michael Parkinson to promote the idea on TV.

I'll say this for SAI, they had some great marketing men, including Tony Martin, a Brit who later became marketing director for Abbey Life.

I can only recall the nicknames we gave two others: Kermit, who sounded and looked rather like the cartoon character, and Tubs who was from Madison Avenue and could have stepped straight into or out of the Mad Men TV series.

They decided to open up a branch in Britain and form The Over Fifty Club. (OFC).

Could we publish a quarterly magazine for them?

While in the army I had taken myself off to Vienna University as an extra mural student to learn something about military history and philosophy. Two of my favourite characters were Sun Tzu, the Chinese military strategist, who wrote about the art of war 500 years before Christ was born and von Clausewitz, a Prussian general and philosopher. Two of their dicta have stayed with me and are highly relevant to business.

Sun Tzu advised: *keep your friends close and your enemies closer* and Clausewitz counselled: *abandon your weak positions and reinforce your strengths.*

Whenever we adopted these maxims for strategy we succeeded. When we neglected them we failed.

As I was not too sure whether SAI were friends or foes Sun Tzu seemed to have the answer. Of course we would publish their quarterly magazine and so began another title: *Life Begins at 50*. Contract publishing for other people was much easier than consumer publishing. The profit was guaranteed. Simultaneous with their British operation SAI tried to spread their message through continental Europe and became badly unstuck in France and I believe Holland. Money seemed no object and I was told they were bankrolled by the American insurance outfit Monumental Life to the tune of $3million.

A smart investigative reporter on the *Financial Times* began to run the rule over them suspecting a scam but as PR consultants we briefed him and, although not totally convinced about their motives, he backed off. SAI was just like any other insurance provider or broker: it operated to make money for its shareholders. What gave it the edge were its up to date actuarial figures whereas in Britain actuaries were still using pre-war data. They had not taken account of better health care and a diet that had improved life expectancy.

Another brilliant marketing ploy was the 'no medical examination needed,' just because you were aged 50 or older. Catch 22 was that pay-outs from the policy did not operate until it had been in operation for two years. If you died within two years of taking out the policy your premiums would be returned to your estate with a modest rate of interest. That filtered out those who beat a path to their door because they had been told they had only a short time to live. The policies were also written through Lloyd's of London, which gave an additional measure of comfort. Lloyd's no doubt re-insured with Monumental.

Simultaneous with *Life Begins at 50* they launched the Over Fifty Club. It promised special discounts for members who bought paint, tyres and many other household items. But the key was the life insurance policy. All seemed to be going well in the U.K.

Could we do a similar magazine for a launch in Germany? Jawohl! We set up *Jungbleiben mit Funfzig – Life begins at 50*. Fortunately Anthea had excellent German and French, not to mention a smattering of Japanese. I was due to meet the German partners in Cologne and began desperately brushing up and revising my German from army days. When I met the German directors in Cologne I found they had all graduated from Harvard Business School and spoke excellent English.

JK and I had a simple approach to publishing. We tried to get the best contributors in their various subjects whether it was health, finance, hobbies, gardening, travel or fashion. Good editorial content – one of the cheapest factors - is the key to publishing, so why stint on that, why not have the best? That's one of the reasons why magazines that are editorially run succeed and ones run by accountants, who find editorial content the easiest operation to cut, fail.

With this in mind I contacted Colin Lawson who was the *Daily Express* correspondent in Bonn and had been part of the military government in the post war years. I explained which key figures and specialists I needed and within days I had introductions to German journalists who fitted the bill. Our American friends were impressed and we produced the magazine in England.

At home one evening I took a call from Kermit. SAI had employed an elderly English-born German language teacher to read the magazine who said the language was dreadful. Kermit advised me it would have to be re-done at our expense. Unless it was, SAI would not pay the bill. As my team of German journalists included people who worked for the *Frankfurter Allegemeine Zeitung, Bild* and *Der Spiegel* this was nonsense.

I made this plain to Kermit. Furthermore I told him that unless the bill was paid pronto the English edition of *Life Begins at 50* would remain in the warehouse and not be delivered. Checkmate. We were paid. What had Sun Tzu said?

Monumental Life sent an accountant over to the UK to check on how SAI were spending their dollars. They were not impressed: no more dollars. SAI had not sold sufficient policies. Executives also seemed to be living high on the hog.

The Americans then decided to pack up their tents and go home. However, they had insurance and club commitments that had to be met. Lloyd's took care of the insurance and I took care of the magazine, buying *Life Begins at 50* for £1 plus an undertaking that I would keep it going for five years and provide it free of charge to OFC members whose memberships included one year, two year and three year terms. 'One or two,' had signed up for life. With an issue due out very soon we had to move fast and with a *de facto* agreement in place Anthea went off to their headquarters to obtain the necessary details.

She arranged for the transfer of all club members' details to be delivered to us in five filing cabinets and also surreptitiously picked up a small black notebook containing details of about 500 life members. I knew then how Bletchley had felt when they got their first Enigma machine. Anthea would have made a wonderful intelligence agent.

I flew to the United States where I met Walter and a dozen or so of his team at their plush headquarters in Cherry Hills. The atmosphere was not too friendly. We thrashed out heads of agreement. Walter said there were only a handful of Life members. 'You've gotta take the rough with the smooth.' Nobody at the table contradicted him. At the end of an exhausting session I typed out what we had agreed and we signed two copies: one each. I had agreed to take over their UK company, but the only liability was to continue the OFC and I would advertise the OFC Life policy four times a year receiving commissions due.

A lift back to the airport? No chance. I called a cab.

Back in the UK we merged *Life Begins at 50* with *Choice* so OFC members were happy to receive a monthly and more interesting magazine. I was happy, for at a stroke we had put on 25,000 in circulation, most of whom stayed with us, and increased the advertising rate by a third. We had also improved the age profile of the title.

When Casson Beckman, my accountants, went through the material supplied by SAI we were able to present accounts that matched our aims and objectives and gave us £750,000 of tax losses worth about £75k.

When SAI's London lawyers got around to sending us a contract I found that everything agreed in our favour had been omitted and everything in favour of SAI included. I ignored it. A second copy arrived after a fortnight. I sent it back with a terse note and a photocopy of the heads of agreement signed in Cherry Hills. Silence. We sent out a second issue of the merged titles. Under the masthead *Choice* were the words: Incorporating *Life Begins at 50*. Walter had left one representative in the UK but he was forbidden to come and see me on his own. By now we had entered all details of OFC on to our system together with their renewal dates.

Eventually Walter came to London and stayed at the five star Berkeley Hotel. A meeting was arranged.

'Are you going to sign this deal or not, John?'

'Yes, Walter, I'll sign it now but I want you to know that in Cherry Hills you and your team were wrong when they told me there was only a handful of lifetime members for which I assumed liability. Your team knew there were 500 or so. So did I.'

'And what would you have done then?'

'I would have asked for a reverse consideration of £10,000, you would have offered £5,000. and we would have settled on that.'

'OK, John, £2500 now and another £2500 if you are still going in three years time.'

We shook hands. Friends again. More than that, we ran a double page spread for the Over Fifty Life policy four times a year for which we received 80 per cent of any first year's premiums written as commission. It matched about the same yield as two pages of advertising.

The workload was building up. JK was editing six magazines, his wife was proof reading at a prodigious rate and June was finding that invoicing was occupying more and more of her time. When Kins came home and asked her to make some costumes or something for a school Christmas play because 'she didn't go to work like other mummies,' she didn't know whether to laugh or cry. We needed more people.

Deadlines all my Life

CHAPTER 14

Up there with the Lord Mayor's show

To handle subscriptions and all the bookkeeping that entailed I set up a satellite office in East Grinstead a mile or two from where we lived. The rent was cheap and the quality of local clerical staff good. They were a super bunch of women and indispensable when we computerised our 60,000 subscription list. It went without a hitch because we ran the old-fashioned system and the new one side by side for three months until we were sure the new one was ok. It wasn't an easy task but the Institute of Directors provided a supportive consultant who also tried to educate me in the use of computer information as a marketing tool. I learned a little but not as much as I should have done.

On school holidays the girls would help out, even taking part on a float we entered for the Lord Mayor's Show. They brought their friends along who were equally at home in the City of London as they were at the Greyhound Derby. The Lord Mayor of London had taken Age Action Year as a theme for his term of office.

We helped him to raise £5million and put him on the cover of *Choice,* together with Kins, who had a new dress for the occasion.

She asked the Lord Mayor about his ceremonial tri-cornered hat and he told her he kept his sandwiches in it. Tony Marshall, a photographer from the *Telegraph,* took the charming picture.

Every friend we had was exploited or pressed into service one way or another. Norman Giller, for example, joined the fray with an excellent picture and *Choice* cover story on Eric Morecambe, 'Laugh your way out of a heart attack.'

Our next appointment was Paul Bach who had been one of my reporters at the *Stratford Express.* He took over the hotel magazines from John and was a real live wire. He had earlier established a typesetting bureau after quitting journalism but new technology soon put him out of business and Barclays foreclosed on his house. We gave him a lifeline.

A little later Saga came a-knocking at our door. The travel company had been started by Sidney de Haan and proved a winner with holidays geared exclusively to our 50plus market. JK and I took the train to Folkestone for a meeting with one of Sidney's sons, Roger. To be fair, we did not appreciate the scope of a tie-up and were a little underwhelmed. A major sticking point was that Saga would have to be the exclusive holiday advertiser.

This would have the effect of wiping out our existing travel advertising which was running near £40k a year. I was uneasy about this and Tony Weller, my advertisement director, would have had a fit. He had a hard enough time keeping up with my unreasonable (as he saw it) expectations without ditching a sizeable chunk of existing revenue.

The sting came a month or two after we rejected Saga's overtures. Paul Bach resigned to launch *Saga Magazine*. We had just had our annual editorial conference at Gravetye Manor Hotel, a delightful four-star venue near Gatwick Airport. We used to gather there once a year on a Friday evening with wives and girl friends invited, have dinner and meet on Saturday to plan the year's twelve issues.

Those not involved in the magazines were free to wander the grounds and enjoy the hotel amenities before we met for dinner in the evening. The event closed after breakfast on Sunday morning. These meetings were hugely productive. The plans could be changed in the light of events or better ideas but at least we knew where we were going.

Paul had been a key figure in these meetings. I tried to talk him out of resigning but he stopped me short. 'Don't offer me more money John because you cannot match it. They've offered me a house in Folkestone and I have to think of the family.'

Regretfully we shook hands. He was to make an incredible success of launching *Saga Magazine* but somehow it never impinged on *Choice*, despite him using many of our ideas. Nobody since Paul has run *Saga Magazine* with the same élan and imagination.

Family events were going well and our caravan holidays led to another magazine opportunity. We had bought a little Ace Airstream four-berth caravan and whizzed off on holidays to the New Forest, Southern Brittany and Austria on the shores of the Worthersee at Klagenfurt. British troops Austria had long gone. Howard had a two-man tent. There were always adventures, fun, mini crises and a build-up of memories. These helped me to appreciate our children and to wind down. June made sure I didn't dare call the office. In any case, I had total faith in JK. I could trust him with my life, not just the business.

We joined the Caravan Club. As one of 250,000 members I received their magazine and a copy of the accounts. The magazine was costing around £100,000 p.a.

Thanks to Bill Lowe, a fellow early morning commuter from East Grinstead to the City, and later to become my stockbroker and good friend, I wangled a meeting with the chief executive, Donald Chidson. His headquarters were in East Grinstead.

He waited for me to open. 'How would you like to save £100,000?'

That got his attention. We had a lunch or two, I explained the black art of publishing and within a short space of time we became publishers to the Caravan Club and did indeed save the Caravan Club that sum with selected advertising and a much better product.

Our clutch of hotel magazines was impressive and we got on well with the marketing director of Rank Hotels, Robert McGregor, who had fought with the Glosters in WWII and Korea. June and I took a break at the Romazzino Rank Hotel, a plush venue in Sardinia, part of the Costa Smeralda development initiated by the Aga Khan. While there I discovered Pevero golf course, a stunning achievement by America's leading golf course architect, Robert Trent Jones. It was a short walk from the hotel.

I knew that Rank's problem with the hotel was the short season that lasted only from mid May to September. I asked the manager why he didn't run golf weeks for a month before the season officially opened and for a similar period at the end, but he had no idea what I was talking about. He would seize on any idea that that made the hotel more viable. Could I tell Bob McGregor and his management in London about the scheme? Indeed I did and he picked up the idea with enthusiasm. Before long the great Dai Rees was hired as professional, the event advertised and a planeload of happy golfers introduced to the hotel and golf course. We enjoyed holidays in Sardinia for several years. As I stepped off the plane at Olbia airport on the first golf trip a Scottish voice behind me said: 'You're THAT John Jenkins.'

I blinked in amazement. 'And you're THAT John Burns.'

He had been my predecessor at *Golfing Magazine* and had left, become a professional golfer, and played the Tartan Tour in Scotland. He had had moderate success but he scored a huge achievement in founding and marketing Ryder Clubs. He was so successful he had sold the company to Ranks for a reputed £3million. At the time, Ranks flush with cash from their deal with the American Xerox Corporation, were hell bent on diversification and the acquisition trail.

Rank Hotels selection of Dai Rees to lead the teaching was a stroke of genius. I had only ever seen him play at the end of his career when he was past his best and infuriated that he could no longer play the kind of attacking golf that had made him one of a select band to captain a successful Great Britain Ryder Cup team against the United States, before the event became Europe against the USA.

He would charge around the course in his buggy playing six holes with each four ball and then double back to pick up the next group. In this way everybody had a chance to play with him. He was also an excellent teacher, a skill not given to many tour professionals when they cease competitive golf.

I am probably biased because with Dai in attendance I could not hit a bad shot. His comment on my golf: 'You should be ashamed of yourself playing off 11.' Apart from golf he would fill in as a fourth for bridge, dance with anybody and generally be the life and soul of the party, without the downside which that description often implies.

Who should we see dining at the Romazzino on one of our visits, but Ken Fleet, the City Editor from the *Telegraph.* Carlo, the headwaiter pointed him out and asked if I knew him. Ken was dining with a sensational blonde and I sent over a couple of brandies at the end of the meal.

As Carlo explained where they had come from, Ken looked over in astonishment.

The blonde, called Marilyn, was not Mrs Fleet, and apparently she had come just to caddy for Ken but seemed to me quite new to that job as her very short shorts were little protection from the scrub as Ken sprayed balls deep into the rough. She must have improved, for several years later I bumped into them in Orange Square, Marbella, where Marilyn was trying to clean ice cream off Ken's jacket. The Romazzino and Pevero golf course provided a lot of fun over several years.

The next caller at Covent Garden was Pontin's. Mike Austin was their marketing manager and a persuasive salesman.

How would we like to run a themed retirement holiday for our readers at the start of the season in one of their Devon camps?

I didn't see it and I didn't think we had spare staff capable of doing it. Not so JK, our very own Stakhanovite. Within a week or two he had organised speakers, a programme of events and mapped out entertainment with Austin. He also harnessed the energy and input of Hillary. From Austin's point of view he wanted to use *Choice* readers as guinea pigs to open up the holiday camp season early and get staff trained to dealing with people. It was a total success and I had virtually nothing to do with it apart from asking my in-laws to try it and report back. They loved it, as did most people.

Austin then enthused even more and suggested we repeated the trick on the Costa del Sol. That was more difficult. By the time we paid air fares to Spain for speakers etc. there was little profit in it for us.

Pontin's were owned by Corals, the bookmaker, one of several, like Ladbrokes and Hills, I had cultivated as advertisers for *Greyhound Magazine*. One of the more unusual tasks we took on was a theatre programme for a famous Arab girl singer who was hired to give a one-night Sunday show at the Coliseum in Drury Lane. The text had to be in English and Arabic. At first we did not get the quality of typeface right but eventually all was well.

The event was to lure Coral's Arab high rollers back to the casinos for even more fun. It was certainly a great success.

Other more conventional PR exercises, for Allied Irish Banks, included racing at Cheltenham and Epsom and obtaining tickets for an Ireland versus Wales rugby showdown at Cardiff Arms Park when the event was sold out. My good contact, the head porter at the Waldorf Hotel, pulled off that miracle for me – at a price. Our client, AIB, did not care what the price was. Dublin wanted some top clients entertained and that was that.

Public Relations for AIB demanded some strange skills. Gerry O'Mahoney had to entertain an Irish financial journalist and asked JK and I to go along to have dinner with him and the correspondent at the RAC club. As soon as he decently could, Gerry excused himself saying he had another appointment but we could stay and the bill was settled. Our Dublin colleague was quick to finish off the Gevrey Chambertin and suggest we ordered another bottle of the same. JK, with his knowledge of fine wines, did not disagree.

There was also a charity boxing night at Grosvenor House. All black ties and dinner jackets. I was foolishly the only person to wear a white dinner jacket which provided a great deal of fun for my Irish bank managers who kept ordering ice creams from me.

Nevertheless, they gave vital support in bad weather and that was just around the corner.

Deadlines all my Life

CHAPTER 15

The £250,000 gamble

Choice was going well with subscriptions increasing but we were lagging in bookstall sales. Somehow we had to crack that sector of the market. Our content was good and even handed: interviews with people as widely varied as Enoch Powell and Vic Feather, Roy Thomson and Katie Boyle, Warren Mitchell, Barbara Cartland and Frankie Vaughan produced great copy, not the PR censored mush that sometimes happens today with celebrity interviews. The fashion of having a PR consultant sitting in on the interview, vetting what will be said and what will be answered, and seeking an undertaking that the subject will have approval of content and pictures is anathema to me and to JK. Even two-bit footballers try this on today, nervous of their image rights.

Thanks to our vigorous PR campaign we were often quoted in the national Press.

The point about Lord (call me Roy) Thomson's feature was that by the age of 60 he had made a fortune in Canada and then arrived in the UK to make an even bigger one at a time when most people were thinking of retiring. JK did the interview and I went along for the ride. We met in his office in the West End and an assistant said we had only 20 minutes. We left an hour later. Thomson advised us, among other things, always to stay close to our bank. He produced two old-fashioned sheets of quarto notepaper from his desk that contained the full list of his Canadian newspapers and a one-line summary of their results. Most of them showed a return of around 30 per cent but there was one that topped the 50 per cent mark. I asked him if he wanted to sell that one. He roared with laughter. From then on he reckoned we were a couple of ok guys.

Warren Mitchell, who gained notoriety as Alf Garnett in Johnny Speight's *Till Death us do Part* turned out to be totally different to his TV character. He was well read and his leisure pursuits were tennis and playing in a classical string quartet. He had also won many awards for outstanding performances on stage. Nevertheless we had letters from readers wondering why we had put that 'awful man' on the cover. In contrast, Frankie Vaughan drew acclamation – particularly from our female readers.

We were determined to top that 100,000 barrier and I reasoned we needed to advertise on TV to do it. Plans were drawn up. Simultaneously the Royal Mail had imposed two price increases in the year that hit our subscription operation hard, plus a marginal rise in printing paper costs.

This had serious implications which we countered by reducing the page size of the magazine from British A4 to American A4. That saved us 6% on printing paper and 10% on postage. We also combined the December and January issues into a bumper production, offering eleven issues a year rather than twelve, instead of increasing the subscription price.

For many magazines January is an unprofitable exercise whereas the Christmas issue is often the best. We promised a special issue and nobody complained. In fact it gave us the chance to give staff a decent Christmas break.

The only dissenting voice came from Tony Weller our hard-working advertisement director who saw the change in size as a disaster. For a top salesman, and Tony was one of the best, he could be unduly pessimistic. But give him a brief to sell on and he was superb. We were marking the new size with a two-part 80th birthday feature on the Queen Mum. We had a special picture for the cover and the writer was the incomparable Dorothy Laird. I really did lard it up. I had done a presentation to our newsstand distributors, Comag, and placed a record print order of 125,000 (gulp) and backed it with a television advertising programme. Total cost? Around £250,000 – all in, as they say in poker.

Once Tony saw the potential he no doubt added his own spin as he blitzed the London advertising agencies with his team and produced record advertising revenue for the issue.

TV advertising had to be booked weeks in advance and once booked cannot be cancelled. Things may have changed since those days. Nevertheless, supposing the nation's favourite granny departed from this mortal coil before we came out? I called a friend at Lloyd's, the world's biggest insurance set up. According to Lloyd's there is no such thing as a bad risk – only a bad premium.

Could I insure the Queen Mum against a premature death? I explained the situation. They came back to me within an hour. The premium was £1200 and if she died before the birthday issue came out I would collect £250,000. Deal. She lived another 21 years!

With all the *Choice* planning and changes going on we took our eyes off the hotel magazines. A strong £ was hitting the tourist market. Planes which had been flying the Atlantic with 90% occupancy were down to 40%, a figure impacting badly on our hotels and the major stores in London which missed the shopping dollars, yen, D-marks and shekels.

Selfridges, for example, which had been taking double page colour spreads, cut back to a quarter of a page. They knew, like their competitors, within minutes of shutting the doors each day what the take was and how it compared with the previous days, a month ago and a year ago and even what the weather had been on those days.

Our hotel magazines which had been a licence to print money, if I can quote Lord Thomson, overnight became a licence to lose it.

Looking at the big picture how did *Choice* do? Well, but nowhere near as well as we had hoped. Certainly not well enough to justify the gamble (right word) I had taken. I was invited to talk to a meeting of Comag circulation reps after the exercise and I was not happy. I had been north for some reason and changed trains at Stoke. There was a WHSmith bookstall on the platform where a Comag representative was talking to the manager. I waited patiently as he ran through a list of titles. Did they want more *Homes and Gardens* or *Vogue*, or more of this and fewer of that? I waited patiently while he went through the list.

'How about *Choice?*' I asked quietly.

'Oh I think it's late this month.'

'No it fucking isn't. It's never late. I'm the publisher and you are supposed to be doing a special box out,' (extra copies) to outlets. I was in a rage. If I had then committed murder I would have pleaded justifiable homicide, if that plea had been allowed in Britain.

I couldn't wait to talk to a roomful of Comag reps. Their managing director was Phil Harris. Without a note I ripped into them without a four-letter word, without hesitation or repetition for 15 minutes. And walked out in a deadly hush. Phil followed up after I had left, and apparently exceeded my anger.

We were in a financial crisis.

There was a party that night at our old neighbours, Tony and Nina Russell. Nina later said she had never seen me so quiet and preoccupied. Tony had just retired as manager of the Lloyds Bank branch in the Strand.

I asked Tony if he would become a non-executive director and together with our accountant Peter Ohrenstein we went to AIB headquarters in Throgmorton Avenue.

I pointed out that we had already put measures into operation to rectify the situation and had appointed Tony, a recently retired bank manager, to add discipline to our financial controls.

I had sublet a quarter of our office space and reduced the number of company cars.

A deal was agreed in which AIB demanded quarterly audited accounts to see if the measures I had already put in place were working, among other strictures. We had what was, in fact, a stay of execution.

Peter, Tony and I stood under umbrellas out in the rain after the meeting. I was angry at the shackles but they convinced me: 'John, no other bank would have supported you. Make the best of it.'

Looking back, the presence of Tony and Peter on our side of the table and Dermot on the other, were key factors in our survival. *Reinforce your strengths and abandon your weak positions.*

We sold *Greyhound Magazine* to Harry Lloyd, racing editor of the *Mirror*, for £50k and kept the contract to produce it, and abandoned two of the hotel magazines.

We edged up our advertising rates and subscription price. After three months we had exceeded our forecast and I was able to tell AIB that they were not going to get any more expensive audited accounts as they could see from the cashflow things were going well. Furthermore I felt they could reduce the penal rate of interest they had demanded for further support. Tony Russell urged me to get them to release my house from the collateral they had demanded as the next step and that was done. I was his guest at a golf day and won the visitor's prize: a beautiful cut glass set of whisky tumblers. A friend indeed. We had come through the crisis fitter and stronger.

As another friend was to say to me on a much later occasion - you know something about this publishing racket John, don't you? Now, there was even more to learn.

Deadlines all my Life

CHAPTER 16

The incomparable joy of children

The children were growing up fast. June navigated the shoals of our children's teenage angst with aplomb and compared with the horrors suffered by other parents we had an easy ride. Our home was a haven for some of our children's friends and they were always welcome. Discussions on everything went on long into the night on occasions.

It would be fair to say that Howard entered wholeheartedly into life at Trinity, becoming an excellent swimmer, water polo player and athlete. He learned to play bridge, appeared in a school play and took up the clarinet and saxophone in the school swing band. June went to one of their gigs where the boys teased her that she was their first groupie.

However, even Howard would admit that this enthusiasm did not extend fully to his studies although he was offered a place at Liverpool University; not that he greeted the news with any enthusiasm.

211

We talked it over and I suggested he might prefer to try for a short service commission in the Royal Navy or Royal Air Force and if he liked that make it a career. He was the kind of person who would thrive in that milieu.

But people were pushing daffodils down gun barrels in San Francisco and 'peace' was the buzzword among the young, without any clear idea on how we were going to preserve it. Then he said: 'I wouldn't mind going into the merchant navy?' And so it came to pass, as they say in the bible.

He joined Chevron Oil Company as a cadet and attended maritime college and courses at Plymouth and Southampton. At last he had found something to do that he liked and passed out as top cadet, winning the Ellerman Prize. Off he went to sea and progressed through the ranks eventually becoming a captain. There were squalls along the way but nothing that threw him totally off course.

He tried becoming a shipbroker for a short while but that was not Howard's thing. He had always been better given responsibility. Back to sea he went with June secretly easing the way financially. There is no doubt that travelling the world gave him a different perspective on life.

Linnie had won a place at Bristol University, and obtained a good 2-1 degree despite all the distractions. She also played a part in the student newspaper taking on several different roles which included a spell selling advertisements. Thanks to my friendship with Barclays Bank Trustee department I got six half pages for her. To my amazement she rang me to say they could not accept anything from Barclays because of the bank's links with South Africa.

If they accepted that advertising they could be kicked out of their offices in the student union building. So much for tolerance and free speech.

Later, she shocked me by saying she wanted to become a journalist. Surely not? Surely yes. My girls did not need assertiveness classes.

Thanks to Phil Bangsberg, an American friend from *Telegraph* days, she got a start on the Birmingham papers, *Mail, Mercury and Post*: an evening paper, a morning paper and a Sunday paper, where he was managing editor. Tough, but great training. She followed me into Fleet Street becoming a leading reporter on the *Telegraph, Mail* and *Times*, for whom she covered the first Gulf War.

Among her other major stories was the sinking of the Herald of Free Enterprise ferry en route from Zeebrugge to Dover with the loss of 193 lives. The loss would have been much greater had it not been for several acts of heroism.

One Linnie identified concerned Andrew Parker, a former policeman who made himself a human walkway across a stairwell that his wife, daughter and 20 other passengers escaped to safety. He was later to receive the George Medal.

On my study wall I have a copy of the front page of *The Times* dated Thursday March 7th 1991 with a story by Linnie leading the paper datelined Kuwait. She covered the first Gulf War with the RAF Tornado squadron from their base in Bahrain, moved to the Royal Engineers in Kuwait City and then covered Seventh Armoured Division into Iraq until President George Bush senior called a halt to the war. Today she acts as News Editor for the *Observer* on Saturdays.

I had also helped one of her school friends, Lance Price, who won a place at Oxford, to find holiday relief work as a journalist. He joined the BBC, became a political correspondent and then joined Tony Blair's Press team.

Beanie noted how much reliance I placed on Anthea and went to a top secretarial college, the Oxford & County, where she excelled. She became PA to the managing director of a perfume company, before getting married. Later she worked as an estate agent and teaching assistant.

Sally moved from Fonthill Lodge (Smodge) as she called it) to Croydon High School that entailed a 40-mile round trip for June. She often shared the trip with other mothers. At other times she took my pride and joy, a 5.3litre Jaguar Coupe, and raced Erica's mother, who drove a Mercedes, across the top route to Croydon past Woldingham.

This information came out much later, long after the Jaguar had been sold. From Croydon High, Kins went to a sixth form college in Cambridge. This was not without its problems but Beanie proved a great ally in this respect.

We enjoyed life and took in days to Ascot, Wimbledon, Covent Garden and Glyndebourne as birthday treats for June. The essential proviso was that I had to take the whole day off.

As far as June was concerned that was non-negotiable. No going into the office 'just for a few hours.' It was easier to give in than argue with my girls. A slogan on the fridge door proclaimed that *A woman who seeks equality has no ambition.*

Another read: *Do you want me looking good or the house?* Of course it was, like life, not all plain sailing. Cars had problems, horses got tangled in wire, Dalmatian Fro got run over, boy friends were a pain and all this teenage growing up made for never a dull moment.

Many strange things happened. A tree in our little copse, which had been blameless for 50 years, apparently jumped out in front of Linnie's car one day which made the bonnet look as if it had been hit by a hammer. The fact that she was racing her brother home had nothing to do with it.

'Will I have to tell Dad?' said the driver. 'Well, if he looks out of the window he's likely to see it,' was June's wise reply.

Bad news was often filtered through June. Howard, who was blameless in all this, said the damage was nothing and he could find a bonnet. He did.

Just as he was blameless when driving into a parked car while understandably distracted by a pretty girl to whom he had to wave. The owner of the car he collided with was in the hairdresser's, when she should have been parking her car half into the shop so that Howard would not have hit it. Worse was to come. She opened the boot, which now looked as if it needed surgery, and it wouldn't close. Some people have no sense.

One Sunday, I was sitting in the garden after a long stint mowing the lawn and thinking deeply about what was going to win the 2.30 at neighbouring Lingfield the following day, when a man in blue uniform came down the drive.

'Mr Jenkins?' he inquired.

'Yes.'

'Mr Howard Jenkins?'

'No.'

' Can I speak to him? It's about a motoring offence.'

'Well you can in a couple of months' time, constable, he's at sea.'

On another occasion I was following strict instructions about the amount of pony nuts to give a particular animal because the owners were preparing themselves for a disco. As I carefully measured out half a scoop, a packet of cigarettes and matches came into view. I wasn't sure which pony smoked. It couldn't have been Linnie or Beanie because they were only 14 and 15.

It became very noticeable that whenever one of them was in trouble, or likely to get into trouble, the covered wagons were drawn in a circle and the miscreants stuck together. It was often hard to keep a straight face and June and I sometimes dared not look at each other. It was useful on occasions to put the telescope to the blind eye and do a Nelson.

My grandchildren have none of these faults but perhaps I am spared the details as I spared my mother certain unpalatable facts.

Deadlines all my Life

CHAPTER 17

A phone call? Do you want to sell?

My oldest friend and best man, Don Gardiner, had done a stint in the RAF before following a successful career in personnel management. Life was not, however, plain sailing and after parting company with Sime Darby he decided to set up on his own as a headhunter.

I found him an office in our suite and introduced him to my bank, accountant and lawyer. Like all start ups he went through a rough time before things clicked into place. I gave him some moral and actual support when he was engaged to find a batch of senior editorial appointments for a Middle Eastern newspaper. It was a far cry from the days when as nine-year-olds we had a scrap in a junior school playground that cemented our friendship. We had followed each other around from cubs and scouts to school, sharing triumphs and setbacks.

I was delighted to be his best man at his wedding and later to attend his golden wedding celebrations with his charming wife Gina. At the celebrations were his three children, their spouses, several grandchildren and

219

partners. A wonderful legacy and a joyous occasion for Don and Gina. They deserved it.

He eventually made a breakthrough with his new business and realised that Covent Garden was the place to be. The place was buzzing and we were coming up to another rent review. It was going to be substantial as there was now fierce competition for spaces in this rejuvenated part of London.

It was time for serious thought. Why should we be paying a substantial sum in rent to the GLC when we could buy a headquarters for the same money? Tom Eyton had once told me that he had added bricks and mortar to his *Slimming* magazine to enhance the attraction of his company. Quietly I began to look around and found a fine house and outbuildings on the perimeter of Richmond Park. It had a stable block which would convert into offices, a swimming pool, tennis court and the house was more than big enough for John Kemp's family and mine. It could be divided sensibly.

Whether we would have had to, or been able to retain our own homes was not discussed. I lived 30 miles south of London and John lived about the same distance northeast of the capital. This meant we socialised little outside work and whether living in the same address would have posed problems was not a factor we were far enough down the line to consider. We had rented a company flat in Bryanston Square, behind Selfridges, and spent occasional nights and weekends there: a perfect *pied a terre.*

The principal thought was: how many staff would we lose, if any, by the move? The solution to that was a mini-bus pick up from Waterloo and Victoria stations: a sensible arrangement for most staff. We reckoned we could keep the key players.

A phone call out of the blue put that situation on hold. It came from Geoff Stott, an executive from Emap which published newspapers and a growing clutch of magazines. They would like to buy us, and we arranged a lunch. Security was all and only JK and our accountants knew.

For reasons that I cannot remember John and I thought that if they were prepared to top the £1million mark we would sell.

Emap, it stood for East Midlands Allied Press, had begun as a newspaper publisher and grew organically and by acquisition to become a front-line publisher of 165 popular magazine titles. Chief among them was *Motor Cycle News.* Others included *Smash Hits, Just Seventeen, Elle* and *PC User* and a title on gardening. They were also into radio and later television. Geoff Stott came down to our cottage for dinner one night and he quizzed Kins on her views regarding *Smash Hits* which she bought regularly. He was impressed.

The management reflected the type of company it was. Chairman was Frank Rogers, a former *Daily Mirror* director, and the company was run on a day to day basis by two relatively young tigers: Robin Miller, an editor with elbows who had been a success with *Motor Cycle News* and David Arculus, an MBA graduate from the London Business School, more a strategic planner and thinker. Stott was their gofer and mightily ambitious. These four represented a formidable management team. Other members of Emap management were less impressive. Hidden in their balance sheet was an undervalued stake in Reuters from which the company later made a huge profit.

We agreed that our talks would be confidential. I didn't want my staff worried and Emap didn't want anybody else to begin a bidding war.

Things didn't work out that way and Ron Chilton of IPC appeared on the scene. We tried to keep that confidential but in the world of journalism that was a forlorn hope. I managed to upset Ron and Robin. One thought he had a verbal agreement that if we ever sold we would contact him and the other that we had broken confidentiality. I soothed both egos as well as I could.

Ron, beset by union problems, wanted to turn IPC into a collection of de-centralised publishing groups. JK and I would continue to run *Choice Publications* and four or five other titles he suggested. One had tremendous potential. Another was a dead duck. The sticking point came when I said we would want an IPC shareholding as part of the consideration. That was a non-starter as IPC feared Robert Maxwell was building up a stake prior to an attempted take-over offer. Instead, they offered loan notes that didn't have the same appeal. Emap said we could take any amount in shares if we liked and that clinched the deal.

To make doubly sure they handed over a chunk of change before the final price was agreed. Despite this gesture of good faith – or was it handcuffs - their accountants were crawling all over our accounts. They had three people on the job and their aim was obvious: every £ they could knock off our debtors (profit figure) saved their client £5.50 for the eventual price had been agreed at a 5.5 multiple of pre-tax profit. I gave up running the company and spent all my time on credit control, chasing debtors with the finesse of a hungry Rottweiler.

In the end Emap accountants didn't cover their fee. I had told Robin Miller that there were no skeletons in the cupboard, only bouncing babies and that proved to be the case.

By now I was impatient with the delays. I phoned Geoff at 6a.m. after a sleepless night and told him that the deal was off if he could not complete asap. I reckoned we could repay Emap's first tranche. He had a team together pdq and we all met at Casson Beckman's office: lawyers, accountants and executives. In two hours the deal was done and Geoff said he would treat us to lunch at Odin's. Fine, but to his embarrassment, in the rush he had forgotten to bring his credit cards, and I picked up the tab. I could afford it. We had topped the £million. Anthea asked me how we had got on with the final round of negotiations? 'We won 4 – 2 but it should have been 5-1.'

'Well, you would say that wouldn't you?' Not a bad judge.

I had three months to do as a handover period and stupidly felt I had given away my baby. It was totally irrational. Emap asked me to identify other takeover targets and outline how *Choice* might be developed.

Choice was essentially middle class and aimed at a population which could reasonably expect a decent company pension in retirement. I felt there was room for a quarterly *Executive Choice* aimed at senior management and another magazine with a lower profile similar to that served by Age Concern and Help the Aged. They discarded the first idea, for which I produced with JK and my Art Director John Birch a beautiful dummy, but ran with the second. They made a huge success of the second with *Yours*, thanks to an editor who understood and brilliantly defined the market.

My feelings were so mixed at leaving *Choice* that I nearly did not attend the farewell party Emap staged for me at the end of my hand-over period. June made me see sense and we had a great night aboard a boat on the Thames, complete with jazz band.

224

I handed over the PR clients to Paul Thomas, really as a thank you for introducing us to the contract for producing the British Midland Airways magazine.

Don asked me to join him in the executive recruitment world but I had worked non-stop for ten years and felt like a break. I also rejected several other offers apart from staying on with Emap as a non-executive director that involved four meetings a year: not that anybody was interested in anything I had to say.

One of the bouncing babies I had not mentioned to Emap included the Caravan Club magazine. The reason was simply that we had not yet included it in the year's accounts under discussion so its importance was minimal to the actual profit figure that was the basis of the negotiations.

I felt it really was a big bouncing baby for Emap to nurture. They had an impressive record with *Motor Cycle News* and certainly understood the market. As Emap's accountants started to try to squeeze and squeeze our figures I attempted to counter this by pointing out what a valuable asset the Caravan Club magazine was and we should probably have an additional consideration (i.e. more money) for handing it over. My view was naïve. That should have been raised at the meeting where heads of agreement were drawn up.

After a heated discussion on this point Emap agreed as a *quid pro quo* that June could keep her company car rather than hand it over with the rest of our assets.

I had made a grave error in believing I could up the ante after our agreement but Emap made a bigger one in not developing the Caravan Club link.

Another mistake that Emap made was in thinking they could develop *Choice* as a successful bookstall title to the neglect of subscriptions, which was understandable bearing in mind their record trade sales with other titles.

In essence they misunderstood its unique selling point and its tie-up with the PRA. In fact the PRA allowed Emap to buy out of the deal that I had re-negotiated up from 1p a copy to 1.5p. Poor decisions from both camps.

To be fair to Emap, they did ask me what I wanted to do? I could stay on and run *Choice Publications*, join their management team or even, I suspect, remain an active consultant.

I had, however, run my own ship for ten years and needed a break. For the first and only time in my life I had what I thought was more than enough money. I had taken a portion of my share of the sale in Emap shares at a marking price of 70p. They were to peak some years later at £17. I had made a mental note to sell some at 100p, some at 150p and some at 250p, which I did. When I make mistakes they certainly aren't little ones, but this is all with the benefit of hindsight. My immediate thank you to June was a full-length mink coat but somehow I think the first two dresses I bought her in Leytonstone were a bigger thrill.

Deadlines all my Life

From here on I was to learn some painful new lessons. The next ten years were going to be very different.

Deadlines all my Life

CHAPTER 18

Unused to a life of idleness

I was 50 years old, in the enviable position of doing what I liked and had enjoyed reasonable success as a journalist and publisher. What was I going to do now?

In truth, I didn't know. I enjoyed a lot of things in life: my family, friends and a variety of interests ranging from golf to theatre, horse racing to the stock exchange. There were a lot of decisions to be made and I bungled most of them

First June and I had become names at Lloyd's. More of that later.

Then I set off around the world, taking in Hong Kong, Singapore and Australia. It was good to have a drink and a meal or two with Phil Bangsberg and Bill Chiles who had gone east. I found Hong Kong particularly fascinating and tried to buy the *Hong Kong Standard* which ran a distant second behind the dominant but flabby *South China Morning Post.*

The Standard was owned by Sally Aw, who had promised her father that she would keep the title going despite its losses. She could well afford it as her Chinese language papers were hugely successful, particularly the one devoted to racing; very big in Hong Kong. There was no way Sally Aw would sell.

As a member of Royal Eastbourne Golf Club I had reciprocal membership with Royal Hong Kong and that was an added bonus, not only for the privilege of playing golf there but also of staying in their clubhouse accommodation, easily the equivalent of a reasonable hotel. Moreover it was available at an acceptable price.

Even the food would bear comparison with the Berkshire or Walton Heath. There was a full Chinese menu plus European dishes.

Partnered with a local professional in one of their pro-ams we finished third in a field of 40. Tipping was banned at the club, I believe because of mega rich Chinese who would then snaffle all the best service.

Anybody found tipping could lose their membership according to club rules. However, when I walked half a step ahead of my caddy with dollar bills folded in my hand they disappeared faster than a conjuror's trick.

Another bonus from Royal Hong Kong was a box at the famous Sha Tin racetrack, presided over by a retired police superintendent.

I remember my father telling me he had shared a table at Belmont Park track in New York while on leave from the navy where the police chief tipped him four winners. My man managed two winners and I found two more on my own for a highly profitable evening.

I also had time to have a suit made, beautifully cut with three fittings, all completed in a week. I wish it still fitted. The tailors however, on learning that I was going to the track again, put down their chalks and scissors, produced the Hong Kong Chinese equivalent of the *Racing Post* and proceeded to tip me four losers. I told them not to give up tailoring.

Phil Bangsberg introduced me to a lively group of American financial journalists who invited me to a barbecue on Lantau Island. On top of a peak was a huge, disused, rusted mineshaft wheel. We knelt before it and asked: 'Tell me great wheel, what is the secret of investment?'

Confucius says: 'Buy low, sell high,' came the message.

On to Sydney where I also enjoyed the Australian way of life and thought that if I had discovered it earlier I might well have emigrated. Bill and his wife Margot made me welcome on both occasions I visited Australia. He got tickets for June and I to see the Test Match at the Sydney Cricket Ground, fixed up squash at the Sydney University complex, introduced me to Bondi Beach and lent me his car to explore.

We took in a beautiful little resort called Mollymook about three hours drive south of Sydney and detoured to make a pilgrimage to Don Bradman's birthplace at Bowral.

At the SCG the Aussies on the Hill had a big banner saying: IF THE POMS ARE BATTING DON'T SEND THE TAXI HOME.

As the MCC stumbled to 20 for three wickets with McDermot bowling like an untamed hurricane that looked good advice. Mike Atherton and John Crawley rescued the situation with 174 runs for the fourth wicket. It was a great day out. The Poms had not lost their fighting spirit.

No trip to Australia is complete without a visit to the Great Barrier Reef and I had a marvellous week on Dunk Island, visiting the reef by plane, yacht and motorboat. A lightning transport strike seemed likely to maroon me on Dunk Island but for 200 dollars a pilot of one of the little craft which flew visitors over the Great Barrier Reef agreed to fly me to Townsville. There were four seats in the plane and within hours I had sold the other three for 60 dollars each and handed the pilot $240. He got us to Townsville with 20 minutes to spare to catch the last plane to Sydney for 48 hours. For part of the trip he let me fly a bit of straight and level. Well, it was supposed to be straight and level.

Another vivid memory from Oz was Boxing Day on the water in Sydney Harbour to watch the start of the Tall Ships race to Hobart. Bill and Margot were so generous. After that we went across the harbour to

Watson's Bay and to Doyles, a magnificent fish restaurant.

Back home there were more pressing matters. I could face a huge tax bill and decided - at June's suggestion - to live in Spain, although this meant leaving her and Sally in the UK.

The three of us had been to Spain and bought a spacious three-bedroomed apartment in San Pedro, on the edge of El Paraiso golf club. I became a tax exile on the Costa del Sol and the family would come out during college holidays.

Not only was the Costa del Sol a haven for tax exiles it was also known as the Costa del Crime for many criminals from Britain set up home there to preserve their ill-gotten gains.

Among them were: Charlie Wilson, Ronnie Knight, Freddie Foreman, and many others. There were also a good sprinkling of accountants and lawyers who had cheated clients and were on the run. To add international flavour many Dutch and German crooks joined the throng. As long as they kept themselves to themselves the Spanish police and Guardia Civil turned a blind eye to their activities.

The Spanish, too, were enjoying a new sense of freedom with Franco's regime over and a monarchy installed. As one Spanish friend, Antonio Castillo, joked to me: 'Under Franco we had no democracy, no drug problems, no strikes, no crime and few tourists. Now we have democracy, drugs, strikes and plenty of tourists.'

Despite this reputation the Costa del Sol was also home to thousands of honest Brits who had made a success of business and retired to enjoy life in the sun.

Nevertheless, in some ways the Costa del Sol had much in common with Las Vegas. Marbella, the undisputed capital of the area, enjoyed boom time. It had been fuelled by the British money, then by Arabs and recently the Russian mafia.

For the first time in my life I had no project or business or timetable to follow. It was a culture shock for a confirmed workaholic.

Like most expats on the Costa we made an occasional pilgrimage to Gibraltar. On one occasion June paid £40,000 for an apartment, which was under construction. It was duly finished on time but the custom then was that the kitchen was not fitted. She spent around £600 on sorting that out and put it on the market for £50,000. In next to no time the flat was sold at full price and we met the purchaser – a newly arrived deputy manager for Lloyds Bank in Gibraltar. Imagine the pleasure of walking across the road to bank the proceeds in his branch. One can only cherish such moments.

After six months I began to realise that being able to play golf every day and go swimming and out for a superb meal was not enough. I became captain of the golf club and that took up a good deal of time when I led a group to fight off an attempt by Wimpey's to water down our rights after they had taken over the complex from a British entrepreneur, Alan James. Being a golf club captain in Spain was not the same as holding the office in the UK. It could be a full-time job if you allowed it to be.

Many of the members seemed unaware of normal golf club etiquette so we explained the rules. Shirts with collars and no jeans was a first step. But what do you do with a stunning Dutch lady who swapped elegant designer jeans for a mini-skirt not big enough to work as a lampshade? She asked me if the skirt was suitable.

I recalled the lines of George Canning who wrote:
In matters of commerce
the fault of the Dutch,
Is giving too little and
asking too much.
And wrote the following:
In matters of etiquette,
the fault of the Dutch
is wearing too little
and showing too much.

I did have a great band of helpers and we continued to run successful pro-am tournaments which attracted top professionals, including the incomparable Tony Jacklin, then at the height of his Ryder Cup fame, and many famous personalities from sport and showbiz. Don Revie, Fred Trueman, Bob Wilson, Jimmy Tarbuck, John and

Maureen Garner, Brian Rose, Peter Roebuck among others were visitors.

Fred Trueman was a star turn but sometimes a little careless with his scorecard. The committee decided that in any competition he would be paired with a member of the committee. I drew first turn and for eleven holes we were daggers drawn. Then we found we had a common dislike: Geoffrey Boycott. I don't know what inspired Fred's dislike but it was deep. For my part I knew Boycott had been unnecessarily rude to my daughter when she was assigned to cover a book signing of his autobiography. Once Fred and I agreed on something he was as good as gold. 'Reet, John lad, there's a few cheats in this club but thee and I'll soon sort them out.'

Fred was not everybody's favourite but when his old pal 'George' Statham was in trouble the first man to organise a benefit for him was Fred.

One visitor to El Paraiso whose company I enjoyed was Brian Mayo. He had lost his legs after licking a ball picked up from a green that had been dressed with a weed killer containing paraquat. Taking Douglas Bader, the wartime fighter ace, as his inspiration, he taught himself to walk and played golf off a handicap of nine. He also built Bryn Meadows golf course in Wales and held a tournament to raise funds for the Douglas Bader Foundation. Many notable sportsmen in Wales plus several comedians and musicians entered to ensure it was a success. Boys with autograph books had a field day.

Brian was a more than generous host and a brave man. While at his course in Wales I took in a visit to a coal mine. I gave silent thanks that my father's family more than a century earlier had left Wales for London.

I also thought it a nice idea to write a novel or two. Many journalists from Hemingway to Les Thomas (The Virgin Soldiers) had successfully trod that path. Why not me?

I had two goes: the first was faction in the Freddie Forsyth style of *Day of the Jackal* where I took an historical fact and embroidered it to become fiction. In effect, by the time I had finished the book, the surprise ending I had devised was overtaken by the truth. The other book still needs to be finished. Perhaps I'll get around to it some day.

These were all symptoms pointing to the fact that I had no real task in life. Sabbaticals should last only so long and mine was over. Or, to put it another way, I had retired too young.

In the UK I had met Bob Brand, advertisement director of *Golf World*. He put a group together to buy *Golf Illustrated*. Investors included people from Hong Kong and a charismatic, mystery Frenchman based on the Costa del Sol, François Perdrix. I took a 10 per cent stake in the venture and wrote regularly for it, apart from contributing to odd titles on the Costa.

Bob did not play to his strengths. He was an outstanding advertisement salesman, but relinquished that role to become what he thought was a publisher.

The magazine was eventually sold and at least we got our money back. During our ownership the magazine had taken houses at Turnberry (1994) and Royal St. George's (1995) where we had a great time watching the golf. At Turnberry I met Gary Player whose book I had serialised while at *Golfing Magazine*. Gary was one of life's eternal optimists: 'The harder I practice, the luckier I get,' was his belief. He had more sayings than the book of proverbs and the golfing hacks who covered the tournaments would often pre-empt him by asking: 'What's your success due to this time Gary, your belief in God, your ability to practise or your nuts and fruit diet?' He took it all in good part.

As the months went by in Spain, one idle day after another began to pall. Bill Lowe, my stockbroker friend suggested I should open an office for him on the Costa del Sol but that sounded too much like a tie and I did not feel I could commit to an eight hour day five days a week. I'd had a few successes with shares and currency speculation and this was the second time in my life somebody had suggested I became a stockbroker.

My currency dealing involved changing sterling into dollars, then into Danish krone and converting back again when a profit showed. All went well for about three months and I showed a profit of £30k. Then the tide turned. Half the profits disappeared almost overnight and I learned that watching the rise and fall of three different currencies 24 x 7 across different time zones was no task for an amateur.

All this exposure to golf entered my system like a virus. Why didn't I put a team together and build a golf course? It was a bit like those far off days when somebody said: Why don't we buy a racehorse?

Every Tom, Dick and Paco seemed to be building golf courses in Spain. Some were superb while others were ill-thought out so it was important to do the job properly.

The key to a golf course is to do it hand in hand with property development. Unless you have that element agreed and verified early, don't even buy the land.

On their own, golf courses struggle to make money. Property is the key. A house or villa on the perimeter of a golf fairway carries a price premium of 25%. If you can add ocean views the premium is 50%.

At the peak of the 1980s golf boom on the Costa del Sol a front line plot at Las Brisas, an excellent course and venue for the Spanish Open, sold to pop star Shakin' Stevens for $100,000.

Included in my scheme were friends: Colin Moseley, my predecessor as captain at El Paraiso and Jack Newman. Irish developers Martin Grant and John Whelan (introduced by my old friends at AIB). Architect David Laing, accountant Ian Watson, Ahmed Gemmal,

an Egyptian entrepreneur and Mohammed Nga, Jack
Newman's former partner in Libya; lawyer Ray Murphy,
accountant John Solkhon, (their clients were Martin and
John) and two more Egyptian gentlemen introduced by
Ahmed, whose names I cannot recall. Joe Farr had
shared in the North Sea oil boom.

The sum total of expertise on this board was
formidable. They were all happy with me as chairman.
We had a share capital of £5million committed.

The big task, which fell to Colin Moseley and me, was
to find the ideal site. Eventually Colin found one on the
main Gibraltar – Malaga highway, 10 kilometres east of
Marbella and 40km from Malaga airport. Perfecto!

It's worth a look at the shareholders, in particular the
backgrounds of some. Top of this as a mystery and an
enigma was Mohammed Nga, Libyan by birth,
international by choice, with an American wife who was
kept on a very short leash. He was mega wealthy, owning
property in the USA, Libya, Spain, Switzerland, London
and Italy but often choosing to stay in plush hotels. As far
as I could tell he had owned a ritzy casino and hotel in
Tripoli and transport and construction businesses. Jack
Newman had served in the Libya in the RAF and got to
know him by accident and became one of his managers
and operator of a plant hire equipment subsidiary in
Egypt. Jack also set up his own business there and
became a wealthy man.

Jack, who was one of my original friends on the golf course project, introduced me to Mohammed with the warning that although he seemed charming he could be an 'absolute bastard'. In fact Mohammed turned out to be the one man I should have trusted all the way.

He and Jack had a massive falling out and I did eventually bring them together which involved the kind of diplomacy that could be used to avert the threat of world war three.

A friend of Jack's from Egypt, Ahmed Gemmal, was another shareholder with homes that included a lovely flat in Mayfair, and a luxury villa in the swish Swiss resort of Verbier.

Now we come to the Irish: builders Martin Grant and John Whelan. They had arrived in Britain with their tools in the fifties and by sheer hard work and no little cunning Martin became the second largest private builder of homes in Britain. Working for them were lawyer Ray Murphy and accountant John Solkhon. They were sent over to prove that the deal was no good and the Irish were not going to invest.

Far from that, they not only convinced Martin and John it was a good scheme, they put together a syndicated £250k share themselves in which June had a stake. Then came Ian Watson, a member of El Paraiso golf club, occasional visitor to Spain and an accountant. He introduced architect David Laing, a member of, but not an executive in, the Laing Construction Company.

Finally came Joe Farr, a member of El Paraiso who had made his fortune by riding the property boom in Aberdeen when North Sea oil was discovered.

Laing's had a subsidiary in Spain and an outstanding general manager in Jim Munro. They won the contract to build the course. Laing's had built the first Spanish motorways when the Spanish government could not afford them, (unlike later when they held out their begging bowl to the EU) so Laing's built them in return for the take or part of the take from tolls. Win, win in a sense, particularly for Laing's.

Negotiations to complete the purchase of the land and collect my shareholders' cash from all over the world, is worth a chapter on its own. Suffice to say that Colin backed down and instead of the promised £250k invested £125k at the eleventh hour. The shortfall was taken up.

Ian claimed to have good financial and bank contacts but clearly not good enough and eventually it was Mohammed who introduced me to Aresbank. This outfit was owned mostly by Saudi Arabia and Libya with 10% Spanish investors. At the time Libya faced a US/UK embargo on trade.

Mohammed had first been jailed by Colonel Gaddifi but later released and they became, if not bosom pals, something close. Mohammed also used to entertain Major Jalud who was Gaddifi's number two. This involved all night sessions in Regine's nightclub and very early mornings aboard a huge yacht in Puerto Banus marina. This included a battery of 'hostesses,' funny smelling cigarettes and coloured little pills that looked like Smarties but didn't taste the same. Although I'm sure Mohammed laid on this entertainment I have to say I never saw him take part actively in any part of it. Neither did I, but not so our esteemed guest and his entourage.

In retrospect the whole episode takes on a surreal aspect. We were invited to meet the chief executives of the bank in Madrid which involved them hiring the top room at an exclusive restaurant followed by a visit to the latest trendy night club at which, during the disco cacophony, a Mr Zinatti of the bank and I agreed on a loan of £5million with an interest rate of 3.5% over Mibor, similar to Libor, after I refused 4.5%. Mohammed, Jack and I went straight from the club to the airport and caught the 7.30a.m. plane back to Malaga from Madrid. Now, it was all systems go for the Santa Maria Golf and Country Club.

Not quite. The agreement on the loan was to be signed locally and the collateral was to exclude the cortijo, to be refurbished as a clubhouse together with perimeter land for about 24 plots. This was set out in a letter signed by the local Aresbank manager, Linares, and me. If you do business of any kind in Spain, particularly with a bank, get any documentation notarised as soon as possible.

Then began two frustrating years of procrastination by the local authority over planning permission. Various demands were put up but the underlying factor was that we had to grease the right palms. The problem was to discover the right palms as everybody had a hand out. All were prepared to promise that we would get planning permission but none really had the power. Mohammed knew a Saudi Arabian friend who was prepared to buy a chunk of our land for £5million. This was a great offer and I put it to the board, acting as a democratic chairman should rather than follow my own instincts to get things done.

Martin said, 'If he will offer £5m ask him for £6m John, and we'll get £5.5m.' He didn't. He walked away in a huff, apparently insulted. Democracy in company affairs is a much over-valued concept.

To add to our difficulties the local left wing politicians were ousted from office in Marbella and in swept a right wing group led by the then president of Atletico Madrid football club, one Jesus Hil y Hil. He became mayor. To say Senor Hil y Hil had had a chequered career was a massive understatement. But, as a good dictator, he did clean up Marbella, physically, ethically and literally.

As far as we were concerned he opened up with a local radio broadcast to say that the people behind Santa Maria G.C. were all crooks and the previous left wing administration had been bribed by us.

I arranged to meet him and took along our impressive lawyer, Peter Montegriffo, from Gibraltar. The mayor was flanked by three senior town hall officials and a clutch of large scale maps showing our land. Far from paying the previous administration a bribe I said we had agreed to provide a football pitch for local youngsters (a planning gain they would call it in the UK) and then the local officials had changed their minds.

At the word football the whole meeting changed. We spent most of the time discussing the merits of di Stefano, Puskas, Duncan Edwards, Bobby Moore, Bobby Charlton, Dino Zoff, Pele, Hugo Chavez and other great names plus his hopes for Atletico Madrid, and the fact that according to Sen. Hil y Hil Real Madrid were nothing but sons of bitches, a favourite Spanish insult. He said it in Spanish and asked if I knew what it meant. Indeed I did.

Suddenly the whole atmosphere changed: we were men of substance and honour. What did we want?

I countered, what could he offer?

He pored over the map and pointed to a large area to the north designated as 'agricultural land,' although it was scrub and only fit for a few goats.

'That for Marbella,' he said pointing to the agricultural land, 'and that for you with planning permission,' pointing to the rest.

Of course, once he had that land he could change its usage but it was a fantastic result for us. I agreed at once.

At a stroke we had planning permission for 27 holes of golf and 2,000 units of accommodation: villas and apartments.

The intrinsic value of the site was £41million of which I owned 10%. The ultimate value could scarcely be counted. I remembered a certain spiritualist's words on patience:

Determination is the strength that will enable you to pass the barrier of useless thoughts in order to create positive thoughts and to be successful in whatever you wish. It comes from within and its partner is patience. Patience teaches you not to push but rather to wait and appreciate the game of life instead, knowing that nothing remains the same, and everything will change at some point.

My best friends would not say that I was over blessed with patience, more a devotee of toujours l'audace type, but perhaps there was something in the mantra. This was the high point.

Two storms were to engulf me personally and the project. June and I had both become 'names' at Lloyd's of London pledging our funds from the sale of *Choice Publications*. While historically this was a safe, long-term bet with regular dividends accruing virtually without any effort, that august body was to suffer the worst three years in its 300-year history. The first year of losses were covered by our reserves, the second by our stop-loss policy, the third was wipe out. It had been impossible by then to insure against losses.

We used separate Lloyd's managing agents and were members of separate syndicates. My losses through my agent Roberts & Hiscox, although horrendous, were genuine. June's losses had a nasty smell about them as the agent changed hands several times and nobody seemed answerable. When we joined there were around 31,000 names but what we did not know was that 4,000 old names had quietly withdrawn from the syndicates pending legal actions in the USA and elsewhere concerning claims for asbestos. This was exacerbated by policies protecting leasing agreements. Within a couple of years the number of names wiped out or resigned totalled 27,000 of whom several committed suicide.

Simultaneously the British economy nosedived and the wave of retiring Britons heading for sunshine, golf and idleness dried up. In fact many of the expats living on the Costa del Sol upped sticks and went home, leaving 2,000 villas and apartments for sale on the coast.

After a slow start, construction was starting in a big way. Laings were working on the clubhouse conversion and moving earth all over the place to make contours for the first nine holes of the course. They used a D7 bulldozer which could literally make hills out of molehills. A caddy office cum-construction office took place in a converted barn and irrigation channels were dug with an ornamental lake established. The swimming pool was brought back into commission, a couple of tennis courts and a bowling green carpet and putting green laid. The place was starting to take shape beautifully. This part time job of mine had become a full time plus occupation, as it had with Colin who liaised with Laings construction crew.

Peter Alliss, whose copy I had once edited for *Golfing Magazine*, visited the site. Peter was fast becoming the best commentator in the world on golf, a more than worthy successor to the great Henry Longhurst. Nobody captured the essence of the game better than Peter.

He wrote:

Here at Santa Maria Golf and Country Club I'm looking forward to watching and listening to people, admiring the views and enjoying the peace and tranquillity without the hassle of trying to hole that three-footer on the last green to save forking out for lunch with appropriate wines.

This really is a delight, the trees, the comfort, even the gentility which is something missing in life today. To be here and enjoy it will be something very special – the Ryder Room, the Cotton bar, the tennis and the bowls. I am delighted to be part of it.... Santa Maria personifies the very word, style.

Other visitors included John Garner, a former Ryder Cup player and international coach who moved to New Zealand after beating leukaemia. He, and his then wife, Maureen, fell in love with the set up.

248

On one of her longer holidays June and I enrolled for Spanish classes and explored Spain away from the Costa del Sol. We visited the magnificent Granada and Generalife and tried winter sports in Sierra Nevada where the Spanish Olympic skiers were training. We were somewhat below that standard.

We stayed in a flat offered by an architect who wanted to do some work on our golf course infrastructure and villas. It sounded wonderful but when we got there the front doors to the block were off their hinges and an icy wind swept through the building. The central heating didn't work and although there were plenty of logs for the open fire there was no kindling. We solved the problems, had a roaring fire and with the aid of a bottle of whisky kept the cold at bay. It was far removed from the hedonistic Costa.

We also had dinner as guests of a retired Syrian police chief. He offered a million dollars for Kins and 100 camels. I stuck out for pounds sterling instead of dollars but he wouldn't budge and the deal was off. He later introduced me to an investment manager for Saudi Arabia who wanted me to find $100million worth of property in London for an Arab investor. Shucks, just another missed opportunity. Another Swiss based gentleman who seemed obsessed by the Footsie index suggested I might like to buy an island in the Pacific which he had going cheap. Again I resisted, just as June resisted his footsie (small F) under the dining table.

Apart from the golf project we had a water company on site serving 2,000 customers and it soon became apparent that our water level was too low to sustain their demands and also that of a golf course. To our relief it proved a relatively easy problem to solve.

June and I had a holiday in Miami with Joe Farr and his new bride, Pat. They had a house on the edge of a lovely golf course and June had just taken up the game. Everything was going fine until she scuffed an easy shot into a greenside bunker.

I had a near impossible shot to get out on to the green without the ball flying over into a lake bordering the putting surface. With a huge effort I deposited the ball on the green with about a shovel full of sand. That left her a nerve-wracking, downhill 30-foot putt which she holed to win the match! Joe and Pat were generous hosts and we were sorry to lose touch.

Another celebration for June and I was a visit to Lisnave shipyard in Lisbon where Howard was chief officer aboard a new Chevron tanker, the 132,000 ton m/t George Shultz, named after President Reagan's Secretary of State. She had been built in Brazil but as the dry dock was needed, the paint for the hull was put in containers on the deck and she sailed to dry dock in Portugal for the work to be finished.

Howard, all of 36, was undergoing his last voyage as chief officer. He was then promoted captain and given his own command. The captain of the George Shultz,

Ken Miles, had tipped me off that Howard would be the next man promoted to skipper. June flew out from the UK and I drove up from the Costa del Sol. Walking underneath this huge ship in dry dock and going down into her tanks was an unforgettable experience.

As a commander, I noticed then, and again later in the United States, how Howard ran things. Very cool, calm and quiet. It was an impressive performance and we felt extremely proud.

Back in Spain money was going out fast and nothing much coming in. We did, however, have a showpiece clubhouse complete with restaurant and snooker room with two full-size tables.

Cashflow in construction is king and the economic downturn had us stuffed. The last decent price for a front line golf villa plot went in Las Brisas at $100,000. After that you couldn't give a plot away. We could and should have weathered the storm but I had one Dissenting Voice (Mr DV) on board and he soured the atmosphere.

True, even with his best efforts I had 52% plus of the votes on my side, but he had revealed back in the UK that he planned to replace me as chairman. Unknown to him a friend of a friend in his golf club tipped me off. Soon, the plan became apparent. He had an agreement to buy Jack Newman's share and that could tip the balance in his favour.

In the formation of the company, however, there was an agreement that any shareholder who wished to back out had to offer his shares at the same price and in equal amounts to the remaining shareholders.

At a bitter board meeting I pointed out that if this man were to sell his shares outside our shareholders' agreement they would be disenfranchised (no votes). Furthermore, I pointed out, that if that if Mr DV stayed on the board I would resign and they could all buy my shares at a market valuation. I had no intention of serving on a disunited board. I withdrew from the meeting so they could discuss openly what they wanted to do.

After an amount of to-ing and fro-ing Mr DV resigned, I suggested he leave the meeting forthwith and we got on with the business. The downside was that Jack was upset that his share sale to Mr DV at a profit was not going to take place. But as I quoted from the *Godfather*, it was 'only business.' David Laing said he would represent Mr DV's interest on the board. That was ok by me.

In pretty quick succession I flew to Hong Kong, Paris, Rabat, Zurich and London trying to broker a deal to release us from the bank's clutches. I met more villains and conmen than you would find in a Mario Puzzo Mafia story.

They included a former member of the Polish Air Force (alleged) a leading Swiss Banker (alleged) the representative of a French-Moroccan syndicate, a mysterious link to the perpetrators of the Brinks Mat bullion robbery and sundry odd and very odd sods.

Every one had something in common: a big chunk of money up front. Typical was a broker from Belgium living in some splendour in a villa on Las Brisas. He had an office fitted out with state of the art computers, and faxed messages from banks situated in Zurich, including NatWest and Credit Suisse. A svelte assistant in a couture little black dress served coffee from a silver pot.

How much did we need? £14million? No problem.

Well actually there was. I did not intend to pay anybody £250,000 up front. I was, however, prepared to put £250k into an escrow account, to be released once £14m was in our account. Mr Belgian's lawyer could draft the agreement with Peter Montegriffo, our lawyer. That was a non-starter. Later the man was arrested by Spanish police and deported. He had stung another golf course developer for the equivalent of £400,000. Police in Brussels were keen to talk to him about other matters.

Some of these conmen were nothing if not persistent. The French/Moroccan man said that I was too rude to do business with and contacted some of my fellow directors. So off I went to Paris with Jack, Martin and John Whelan. We had coffee in the George V hotel, not far from the contact's office in the Rue du Boeuf. I remember it well because Martin paid for the cab from the airport (£20) and I volunteered to pay for the coffee and basket of croissants - £40! At least they had a laugh.

Even without me at the meeting they could see the set-up was phoney. However, Mr DV was keen to get in on the act and fell victim to the alleged Swiss banker. Again I was excluded from the meeting while Mr DV bustled about flanked by the Swiss contact, his entourage and representatives from Aresbank. It was a glorious moment for him as documents were photocopied, secretaries sent scurrying for papers and I was excluded from all contact.

All went swimmingly until the phoney Swiss banker assumed that Aresbank would make the funds available for him to buy the project. Wrong. The fury of Aresbank officials and the discomfort of Mr DV at the end of the day as my requisitioned office was handed back to me was a joy to behold. What's the word? *Schadenfreude?*

Another problem to contend with were our accountants who had been introduced by Mr DV. They presented me with an enormous audit bill two days before our annual meeting. I said I was not going to pass it whereupon they said they would not sign the accounts. OK, I would move that they should be replaced and would say why.

They had tried the old dodge of charging audit clerk's time as partner's fees. In the face of my accusation and figures they dropped the amount of their bill by £2,000.

They also tried to pin unauthorised expenses on me via my trip to Hong Kong with June. Unlucky. I had my personal credit card showing the air fares and hotel booked. Whose hand was behind all this, I wondered for a millisecond?

In the words of the great General Patton should I have kept Mr DV inside the tent pissing out rather than have him outside the tent pissing in? Neither option was attractive.

Aresbank did make one final attempt to help. They sent a senior manager to London and we all gathered at a room in the Institute of Directors where I was still a member.

Briefly the scheme was that we should increase our share capital by about 20% and they would see us through the essential infrastructure to get some villas built. It was a handsome offer, but just as we all had to agree a share sale and price we all had to agree to raise the capital. What had once worked for me, now worked against me. Mr DV refused and the offer was withdrawn. What with my personal losses at Lloyd's and constant business problems I marvelled that I survived.

In one final attempt at a rescue Ray Murphy engaged a lawyer in Madrid, The three of us went to the bank HQ to meet their team just ahead of Christmas. We finalised heads of agreement and once more I found myself late in the evening typing them out for all to sign.

A few days went by with no sign of a formal document. I phoned our man in Madrid Sen. Prol, who airily told me not to worry, it was the time of the year. 'Yes, I needn't worry. I could go back to the UK for Christmas as nothing would happen until after the

Festival of Kings, January 6th.' But the heads of agreement had not been notarised.

I flew home on about the 21st Dec. Three days later I had a call to say that the bank had arranged a special session of the local court, obtained possession of our site and moved into the clubhouse and offices with armed guards and locksmiths. Happy Christmas. The New Year fight was going to get very dirty indeed.

CHAPTER 19

Some highs and very lows

I could not get a flight back to Spain until January 2ⁿᵈ. Various people were running around like wet hens and I was distinctly *persona non grata* with virtually everybody. The bank had moved into the clubhouse with a locksmith and an armed guard, taken possession and arranged to sell the site on to a group in Cyprus headed by a relative of the chairman of the bank. The whole deal smelt like offal that had been left in the sun rather than put in a fridge. Under an armed guard I was watched and allowed to remove my personal effects.

The court hearing was deemed illegal on my appeal and there were strong suspicions that previous court officials had been bribed.

The bank hit back by converting the sale of the site to the Cyprus group to an option to purchase and went about matters in a more orthodox way.

In their haste to grab everything the bank had, however, overlooked our water company, Elvira Agua, and its 2,000 customers. That gave me an income to brief lawyers, pay around £500,000 to smaller creditors and continue the fight for the better part of a year.

During this time my eldest daughter Lin had a wonderful wedding to Jonathan. Jack, to his eternal credit, flew over to attend the ceremony and celebrations with his charming wife Sylvia. In what should have been an equally happy day for me I was inwardly seething and pre-occupied with events in Spain where two gentlemen from Libya had buttonholed me in Puerto Banus bought me a coffee and suggested none too kindly that I should give up fighting the bank and depart for England. The threat was unspoken, but crystal.

Stupidly I fought on. I had several small victories but was never going to win the main battle for which the only objective was complete re-financing during an economic downturn.

I revealed to the US embassy in Spain how Aresbank might be helping to bypass the US-UK trade embargo on Libya. Certain changes followed at the top of the bank HQ in Madrid. The chief executive, a Libyan, was posted to Bahrain and a Saudi Arabian official put in his place. Saudi was friendly with the USA.

Then came a crunch visit from the Spanish revenue department dealing with insolvency. They pointed out that I was trading illegally with the water company as it was a subsidiary of the main company and thus belonged to the bank. Despite my payments to the smaller trade creditors the water company asset had to be given up to the bank. If I resisted I could be jailed.

I rang Martin Grant and briefed him on the situation. 'You've given it your best, John. You will have to give up. You can't fight a bank.'

I returned home shattered. For two years I was really fit for nothing. Everything I had built up and worked for had gone. I'd even had a good go at wrecking my marriage. Fortunately June was made of sterner stuff.

Deadlines all my Life

CHAPTER 20

Capitals, galleries and bullfights

I should emphasise that I did not spend my entire time on golf in Spain. Cities attract me and Madrid was no exception. On several occasions Jim Munro, the chief executive for Laing's construction arm was my host and at other times I wandered around on my own.

Without doubt the paintings in the Prado made the greatest impression on me. The sheer talent of Goya and Velasquez, not to mention the raw emotion of Picasso had me returning to Madrid.

Until then, knowing next to nothing about painting, I had merely visited galleries muttering ooh and aah at the skill and subjects. I had often discounted Picasso as a clever artist who merely exploited a particular fashion. My friend Jim Ashford had given me a Picasso print of Woman with a Guitar. In a special building I saw for the first time a painting which spoke to me and said more about war than a thousand words: Guernica.

After the horrors of the Spanish Civil War in the thirties Picasso expressed his outrage against war, with

Guernica, his enormous mural-sized painting first displayed to millions of visitors at the Paris World's Fair. It has since become the twentieth century's most powerful indictment against war, a painting still relevant today.

Much of its emotional power comes from its size, approximately eleven feet high and twenty-five feet wide. Guernica is not a painting you can observe with detachment; it triggers a debate in your mind between what is right and what is horribly wrong. This painting challenges to destruction the notion of war as heroic. Why did Picasso paint it?

In 1936 the conflict began between the Republican government and fascist forces, led by Generalissimo Francisco Franco. Hitler sent the Luftwaffe to aid Franco and to perfect their technique. On April 27, 1937, the Luftwaffe bombed the town of Guernica in northern Spain, a place of no strategic military value. It was history's first aerial saturation bombing of a civilian population. For more than three uninterrupted hours, twenty-five bombers dropped 100,000lb of explosive and incendiary bombs reducing the defenceless area to rubble: a practise run-through for the blitz of Warsaw and London. Twenty more fighters strafed civilians trying to flee. The devastation was appalling: fires burned for three days, and seventy per cent of the town was destroyed. A third of the population, 1600 civilians, were wounded or killed.

News of the atrocity reached Paris and reports filled the front pages of newspapers. Picasso, sympathetic to the Republican government of his homeland, was horrified by the reports of devastation and death. After hundreds of sketches, the painting was done in less than a month and then delivered to the Fair's Spanish Pavilion, where it became the central attraction. Accompanying it were documentary films, newsreels and graphic photographs of the savagery of civil war, rather than the typical celebration of technology people expected to see at a world's fair. The Spanish Pavilion shocked the world into confronting the suffering of the Spanish people.

According to local legend, in the 1940s, when Paris was occupied by the Germans, a Nazi officer visited Picasso's studio. 'Did you do that?' he is said to have asked Picasso while standing in front of a photograph of the painting. 'No, you did,' said the artist.

A totally different museum was the Museo Taurino de Madrid, an obligatory call for any aficionado of bullfighting. Among the suits of lights of famous, brave men, and posters of long forgotten corridas, was an exhibition of memorabilia recording the visit of Hitler's deputy, Himmler, when he attended a bullfight staged in his honour. The posters carried a black swastika centred on a white circle in the middle of a red banner. It took place in 1942, the height of Nazi Germany's success. It is interesting that Hitler did not go. In fact after one earlier meeting with Franco he declared that he would rather have all his teeth removed without an anaesthetic than meet El Caudillo again. Just another strategic mistake by the Fuhrer. If he had persevered and captured Gibraltar with Spain's help he would have had the key to the Mediterranean.

As an Englishman in this former sanctuary of fascism I strolled away from the Plaza de Toros in thought to pass a statue honouring Sir Alexander Fleming, the inventor of penicillin, a drug that saved hundreds of matadors from death after being gored. The matadors had paid for the statue themselves. Spain was not an easy country to understand.

Of course bullfighting has declined as football has flourished. It is now banned in Barcelona. Thanks again to a helpful hotel hall porter I got a ticket for a Real Madrid game at the Bernabéu Stadium.

No visit to Madrid in those days was complete without a visit to Horcher's an exclusive, German-owned restaurant. During World War II it was the headquarters of the Nazi Abwehr. On my last visit, diners included several prominent German politicians.

The original Horcher's in Berlin, is, I understand, equally good. During World War II its key staff were exempt from military service and the restaurant also catered for Goering's country estate. Berlin, however, is a capital I have yet to visit.

Jim Munro also invited me to partner him in a golf tournament at La Moraleja in Madrid. Also in our four ball was the British Ambassador, Sir Robin Fearn. At the time Basque Separatists were conducting a bombing campaign against prominent officials, so apart from four caddies we also had two armed bodyguards on our round. (To protect the ambassador, not me). It looked more like a platoon on manoeuvres than a pleasant four-ball.

Robin, who had worked for Dunlop before joining the diplomatic service, was great company and a most unlikely and refreshing figure – to my way of thinking – for an ambassador.

Among memories of Spain is the Plaza de Toros de la Maestranza in Seville, the capital of Andalucia. This city is famous for its wines and bullfights. American John Fulton, an artist as well as a bullfighter, is still revered in the city. Apart from his paintings he has written the best book on bullfighting by a non-Spaniard.

I have his book and one of his paintings.

Hemingway, in Death in the Afternoon, described a *corrida* as 'the only art in which the artist is in danger of death and in which the degree of brilliance in the performance is left to the fighter's honour.'

It's one of life's strange coincidences that years later I met another American author, Barney Conrad, who had also fought in the rings of Spain and had written the introduction to Fulton's book.

I quote from Conrad: *In 1968 I saw Fulton perform at a charity fight. He hadn't fought in months and was up against some good Spanish matadors who had been fighting all season. Yet John was clearly the best. The arena floor was dangerous grass instead of the usual sand and John fell. The bull was on him in an instant and gave him a terrible working over. Somehow he got to his feet, grabbed his muleta and sword and had the crowd cheering. He dropped the animal with a perfect thrust and was awarded the ears and tail.*

And a final note on bullfighting, if you are interested, visit Ronda, in the hills above Marbella where every autumn they hold the *Feria Goyesca* (properly called the *Feria de Pedro Romero*) It celebrates three great names from Ronda's past: the 18th century bullfighter, Pedro Romero; the painter, Goya; and the great 20th century bullfighter, Antoñio Ordóñez. Everybody dresses up in the costumes of Goya's days and it's quite a party.

Other capitals I enjoyed include New York and Paris but I cannot write much new about them other than to say that if it is your first visit to Paris try a trip up the Seine on a Bateau Mouche which leaves from Pont Neuf or Pont de l'Alma. It's like dining in a floating greenhouse and magic at dusk as the lights of Paris flicker on.

The same goes for New York: a boat trip around Manhattan Island, down Hudson and up East River with an Irish American commentator is an education. My father spent two leaves in New York hence, after his account, I was eager to sample as much as possible. He had been the guest of the Singer sewing machine family and was high in his praise for American hospitality. They had one of the last private homes on Fifth Avenue.

Jack Dempsey's bar no longer existed but I tried a few hot spots in Greenwich Village, dined in the Empire State building and enjoyed the city's remarkable buzz.

For vastly different reasons I count a Press trip to Israel as the most memorable place I have ever visited. The whole experience of Israel corrected many impressions and opened new lines of thought, fuelling my natural curiosity on the Middle East, first kindled by the bible and then *Seven Pillars of Wisdom* by T.E. Lawrence. To stand on the spot where the Sermon on the Mount was preached, overlooking the Sea of Galilee, to observe at first hand the chaos in the Temple and to recover from witnessing the experience of the Holocaust Memorial was unforgettable. The Israeli Tourist Board, which laid on a visit to a showpiece kibbutz and a stay in a plush hotel on the shores of the Red Sea, were irrelevant. A simple signpost saying *Bethlehem 2 miles* was much more significant.

Cities are just fine with me, whether Marrakesh or Lisbon, Singapore or Bangkok, Dublin or New Orleans but I think Sydney in Australia and Edinburgh remain my favourites.

The lotus days were over. The bank account was empty and to make matters worse I lost a £76,000 court case to the Inland Revenue. The verdict was wrong – but I was up against a QC and I was reminded of the surgeon who said, the operation was a success but the patient died. Well, I won the argument but lost the case.

Perhaps I should go back into publishing? In my ten years away the scene had undergone a revolution, changing more during that period than it had done in the previous century. I had embraced a personal computer in Spain as a useful tool and had bought one of the first Amstrad machines that made Alan Sugar's fortune, but at a printing exhibition in Birmingham I gasped at what progress had been made by Apple Macs. I was way out of date.

Kins, my youngest daughter had returned from a round the world trip and decided that she wanted to go to university after all. Which she did.

I decided to go back into publishing.

My first visit was to Hambros Bank which had been my main bank in Gibraltar and where I had introduced substantial funds and customers. The sum of £30,000 which I needed did not faze them but without sufficient collateral, which I did not have, they refused my request. I did not have the fare back to Bournemouth. I went to Hatton Garden and sold my Rolex watch. Back in Bournemouth I sold my Mercedes and my Jaguar and bought a Ford Escort.

Now what? I bought a little magazine called *Businesswoman* that was issued free to about 100,000 women through various centres. As part of the deal, Mel Gregg, the owner, agreed to stay on as advertisement director until I had paid the final tranche of the purchase price.

This meant running two offices, one in Pear Street, London (we later moved to Grays Inn Road) and one in Denton, Manchester which was the home of *Businesswoman*. I should have stuck to one set of offices.

Sally joined the team having left university with a degree in marketing.

I thought there was a niche in the market for a short story magazine after Fleetway Publications closed *Argosy* which in the past had been a launch pad for many good writers, but the economics of publishing had changed greatly in my time away. WHSmith as retailer and wholesaler had a stranglehold on the market despite the fact that in my decade away petrol stations and supermarkets had taken to stocking newspapers and magazines.

This was tough on the traditional corner shops and even tougher on small publishers who had to buy shelf space in many outlets, provide copies on sale or return terms and part with 45% of the cover price. Those were the cut-throat terms of supermarkets.

This meant that launch costs had escalated. Furthermore, the introduction of bar coding meant that retail outlets no longer had to bear the cost of pilfering and shoplifting. If a bar code did not appear on the sales print-out then the copy was listed as unsold and the publisher bore the brunt of any stock pilfered from bookstalls and railways station outlets. Back in *Choice* days a **WHS** manager at Victoria confessed that shoplifting cost him £2000 a week. Not any more.

To Mel's credit he kept to his side of the bargain and ran his small adsales team in Manchester efficiently. He had every incentive for the final tranche of the purchase price depended in part on his performance. Looking back at a copy published in 1994 the contributors were impressive with (Lady) Olga Maitland (*Sunday Express*) and Liz Hodgkison (*Daily Mail*) among star names along with a profile on Glenys Kinnock.

The *Reader's Digest* format suited it well and I should have resisted the temptation to increase it to A4 size. The switch did not result in greater adsales and neither did the title make any impact on the bookstalls. To give some idea of the competition it took a budget of £5million to launch *Cosmopolitan.*

Raconteur looked a good bet. The premise was to run a quarterly short story competition and publish the winners in the magazine. Entrants paid £5 to enter. The winner in each issue would receive £500 and the overall winner in the year would receive a gold medal and £10,000. I hired Graham Lord, former Literary Editor of the *Sunday Express* as editor and while he did a good job in many respects he refused to become a partner in the operation. Alongside the prizewinners we published stories by two well-known authors and sometimes a classic by Maupassant or Chekhov.

With the benefit of hindsight, *Raconteur* was launched with an inadequate budget. It needed to grow its subscription sales fast to make it work but that could not be done without substantial funds.

A glimmer of light came when the *European* newspaper, under editor Charlie Garside, agreed to sponsor the gold medal and award. Not only did that underwrite the prize, it gave us welcome publicity. The quality of the stories was outstanding. The early winner of the major prize, Eamonn Sweeney, was spotted by a literary agent who landed a $250,000 book deal for three novels for him.

Fleet Street rallied round with excellent reviews in the national press from the *Sunday Express,* the *Independent on Sunday,* Freddie Forsyth, Jilly Cooper and Laurens van der Post, among others.

The judges for the final prize were: Ruth Rendell, William Trevor and Sebastian O'Kelly (features editor of the *European*). Despite this galaxy of talent I could not make a breakthrough with WHS. The magazine section said it was a book and passed me on to the book department. The book department said that as it came out four times a year it was a periodical and passed me back to magazines. I lost count of the number of times I travelled down the M4 to WHS headquarters in Swindon. They seemed to be in turmoil with low staff morale. In fact I never spoke twice to the same person.

Kins had joined me in the enterprise and Ted Dickinson, who provided me with somewhere to stay in London, put in a couple of days a week editing.

Despite all this, it's fair to say the magazine would have run into profit had the Barclay brothers not bought the *European* and decided quite quickly to close it, which meant we lost our sponsor. I spent many unsuccessful months trying to find another sponsor to no avail. Hopes of continued Lloyds Bank support vanished with the demise of the *European*.

Clearly I had lost my Midas touch and there was no choice but to close the titles and wind up the company: a literary success but a commercial failure.

The death of Jim Ashford, one of my oldest friends, was a severe blow. The Camelot era was truly over. My mother died at the age of 86 after a short illness and spending the final few weeks of her life in a care home as did June's parents. We had bought them a handy little flat in Wareham but a combination of Alzheimer's and dementia ruined their final days. We did arrange, however, for a telegram from the Queen to mark their golden wedding anniversary.

I returned to Dorset where we had a flat and thought I would try starting a PR agency. Helped by Kins I found a couple of clients but the atmosphere lacked the buzz and contacts of London. In my jaundiced view they could not recognise a good PR idea if it jumped up and bit them in the arm or elsewhere.

I sold a couple of good articles for £900 and £1,000 but life did not get any easier. We downsized twice, from our beautiful double flat in Parkstone, first to one in Bournemouth and then to a house in Verwood.

Family news was not great. Howard's career flourished but his marriage fell apart as did Beanie's. Kins had got herself a great job after my company folded and also decided to get married. That, too, did not work out. These things mattered to June and I much more than our financial woes.

I had a commission to write a book on the charity business for Kogan Page and was way behind schedule for providing the manuscript. In desperation I advertised for a secretary and Mary Hogarth applied. She was not the first one interviewed but she was insistent and desperately needed the job. She had graduated in journalism from Solent University but could not get a job on a magazine or newspaper.

With her help the book was completed on schedule during which time I bought *Writers' Forum* and she stayed on to become editor. She was just the sort of person who would have flourished in my days as editor of the *Stratford Express*. She learned fast and worked incredibly hard. She was also fiercely loyal and June and I were lucky to have her as a friend.

The seller of *Writers' Forum* was Morgan Kenney, a Canadian who, unlike *me and m' poetry books*, if I can quote Pam Ayres, had made a fortune from academic publishing. In Canada children have to be bi-lingual and Kenney was the first man to write child friendly language books with illustrations and simple stories rather than pages and pages of unleavened text listing irregular verbs and the like. He told me his best book netted $7 million. That's Canadian dollars but still useful change.

There was a strange and lucky spin off from my book on charity. In my Fleet Street days I had worked occasionally with a small, inspiring design agency in Blackheath, Tully Goad and Partners. We formed a partnership known as Words & Print which did well with what clients we obtained but we lacked the resources and expertise to generate sufficient new business. One of our clients was the South Suburban Co-Op Society which had a switched-on marketing director.

Every time the SSCS opened a new store he would want a newspaper produced that was delivered free to around 100,000 Co-Op milk customers promoting the new event.

The opening ceremony was conducted by a popular TV personality, for example Hughie Green, and the Royal Marines Band was engaged to parade up and down outside the new premises. Thousands turned out for the opening event. At Words & Print we produced the newspapers.

David Goad's wife, Jenny Campbell, was a magazine journalist and we roped her in as Women's Editor. Although Jenny was more Harrods than Co-Op she was a true professional and turned out great copy.

The newspaper played a major part in the store openings and everybody was happy with the result.

W & P ceased trading and I paid off a small bank overdraft. I also stole Tully Goad's designer, John Birch, who joined my team at *Choice*.

Years later, trying to re-build my life, I read a small paragraph in a trade magazine to say that a Jenny Campbell had been appointed as editor of *Candis*. This was a title I had come across while writing a book on Corporate Charity for Kogan Page. It looked a suspect operation and I had made a mental note to follow up with the possibility of a page lead in one of the Sunday papers when I had finished the charity book. I just didn't believe that an unknown magazine had donated more than £40million to charity.

I rang Jenny and was delighted to meet her again. Meanwhile I went off to the Charity Commissioners to check on *Candis*. No scandal whatsoever. In fact the lady at the commissioners gave a glowing account of the work by the magazine and its promoters.

Lunch with Jenny was a delight, particularly as she engaged me as fiction editor to find a suitable short story every month. This ran parallel with my *Raconteur* work. Not so happy was the news that her husband, David, had suffered greatly from ill health and Jenny was now the major breadwinner. They had quit their lovely home and had moved near to the *Candis* headquarters in Hoylake, Cheshire.

The more I learned about *Candis* the more astonished I became at its achievements and as we approached the time when their charitable giving would reach £50million I suggested a book to mark the occasion.

My first suggestion for an author failed to materialise as he tried to get an increase in the fee he had agreed with me by approaching the managing director of *Candis* direct. With deadlines looming I reluctantly took on the job myself.

I wrote how a Liverpool company doctor, accountant Joe Douglas, had lost two close relatives to cancer and vowed to support medical charities through reviving a charity football pool. There were several such ventures at the time and often the promoters were charlatans. Winners were sometimes not paid and charities derived little benefit. The government tightened regulations, got rid of the conmen but as is often the case with hurried legislation made life impossible for the genuine promoters. Joe Douglas took it as a challenge. He had always run a newsletter to keep members informed of the gifts to charity and now he turned that enormous subscription list into an excellent club with a family magazine called *Candis*.

At the time I joined it had 365,000 club members as subscribers, a remarkable success. Jenny had developed into an excellent editor and the magazine was as good as, and better than, many on the bookstalls. Despite starting far too late my book made the deadline for the £50million moment and several thousand copies were sold. Shortly afterwards Jenny decided to retire and the new editor naturally brought in her own team.

Since then the volume of donations to charities has declined steeply and the circulation has dipped by more than 100,00. This mirrors the general decline in magazine sales despite herculean efforts by the marketing team at Hoylake. In an attempt to arrest the decline by embracing bookstall sales the magazine became much more a woman's title rather than a family offering and found itself up against formidable opposition. The move did not succeed.

However, writing about Joe Douglas's achievements put me on the road to biographies. Why he was never knighted for his services to charity while overpaid football managers reap top honours is beyond me.

*   *   *   *

Mary eventually returned to the academic world taking with her a pragmatic, experienced approach to journalism as an antidote to some fatuous academic ideas. She wrote several excellent books and was also responsible for getting me a post as a visiting lecturer on magazine publishing.

June and I visited the United States to stay with Howard and his new bride Sally. They gave us the warmest welcome and it was good to see them so happy. Howard had given up skippering oil tankers and taken a series of shore jobs with Chevron. More than that, he had taken out American citizenship. They entertained us royally with memorable visits to New Orleans and its incomparable bars, such as Pat O'Brien's, surely one of the best piano bars in the world. Unfortunately on my second visit there I thought I had pulled a muscle in my back and was in agony. The problem was not solved until I met Nick Parr in the UK who told me I had a displaced rib and cured the pain with acupuncture.

Certainly the friendliness and hospitality experienced in Mississippi and Alabama showed a generous side of America.

Whether in New York, Santa Barbara (California) the Carolinas or the southern states I always enjoyed my trips to the USA.

* * * *

If at first you don't succeed give up would probably have been a good motto but I stuck to the original one to try and try again. *Writers' Forum* was an ideal title to link with my old short story magazine idea which I re-launched as *World Wide Writers.* London was out of the question on grounds of expense and we took an office first in Poole and then in Bournemouth.

June had taken up golf and joined Bulbury Woods Ladies and I joined Brokenhurst and for several years enjoyed the friendship and banter, so life was not all work and no play. We were keeping our heads above water.

June became captain of Bulbury Woods ladies and enjoyed a memorable captain's day. Great weather, Bucks fizz and a ride around in a buggy for grandchildren Carl and Charlotte. June was never the fiercest natural competitor but she was determined to win the Grandmother's Cup and did so in style by three shots, much to everybody's delight.

With a much lower budget, Spartan overheads and lower expectations we made publishing progress but not enough and not fast enough.

My heart attack in 2008 did not help. I phoned my old friend Ted, who had had heart problems and new valves inserted. 'Put the phone down now and call an ambulance,' he insisted. I could barely look at June for she had suggested the same thing hours earlier.

My thoughts of immortality faded as the ambulance rattled down the A338 to hospital in Bournemouth. The paramedics had put me on oxygen and a drip and eventually I began to feel a lot better. However, they would not turn around and take me back home. 'You should have called us earlier,' they counselled.

Fortunately I recovered but found I had lost the capacity to work non-stop for 16 hours. While I was away, June, my cousin Janet Wyatt and Mary kept the ship afloat. A super girl called Wendy Goodman sold advertising for me from her base in Exeter.

With my health raising problems we tried to re-organise what little resources we had left to protect June should St Peter call me early, as seemed likely.

This principally involved me taking out a chunk of insurance to ensure that June at least had the house in Verwood unencumbered and a little to spare. I also looked to sell *Writers' Forum*, which I had acquired quite cheaply. In the end I took £45,000 for it that did not go very far after debts were paid. A year earlier I had turned down £110,000.

Two more years down the line and June was diagnosed with cancer. It made everything else insignificant.

Nobody could have been braver but I clearly remember the shock when the consultant told us that the cancer had advanced only 10% in a year. I went back to see him on my own. **ONLY 10%?** I knew what 10% compound per annum meant and this was far more serious than we had been led to believe. June had agreed to take part in the trial of a new drug but that proved to no avail. She died at home on March 3rd 2012 and after that not much seemed to matter.

Her funeral demonstrated the way she had touched many people's lives and hearts. Her cancer support group turned out in force, so did her golf club and the friends she had made running the Dorset branch of the WRVS. Veg (Kins' school friend Verity - known to our family as cuckoo) flew back from India for the funeral.

For a while I was in a daze, certainly not thinking straight. My family were hugely supportive and in time friends said I would get over the loss. I don't think you do get over such a loss – you merely learn to live with it. The immediate problems were emotional and financial: one pension instead of two, being one of the blows.

From an emotional viewpoint I had not only lost the love of my life, I had lost one person who never lost faith in me. Two friends also died, Ted from heart complications and Bill Lowe from cancer.

For my 80th birthday the family organised a boat trip on the Leeds to Liverpool canal. In October Yorkshire does not offer bikini weather so we were all wrapped up in sweaters and anoraks. The party had begun in Harrogate at the home of Kins the previous night where everybody gathered, including Howard who flew in from the United States. Consequently on the morning the mini bus arrived to take us to the boat the 'crew' were decidedly hung over. The spread, prepared by the girls, was sumptuous and we celebrated in style, recovering in the wind and rain, from the previous night's excesses. Unforgettable.

A postscript to the Spain fiasco arrived when Ray Murphy wrote to me saying Mr DV was suing Martin Grant for not looking after his interests. This was nonsense and I had kept taped recordings of the board meetings, which showed that at no time had Martin given that undertaking. I suppose that Mr DV did not fancy suing his buddy David Laing. I sent the tapes to Ray and no more was heard from Mr DV.

CHAPTER 21

Why should vocational degrees take three years?

In the year after June's death I clocked up 25,000 miles in my car with no good reason. I could not stay in on my own and apart from survival lacked direction and judgement. Out of the blue an old *Telegraph* colleague, Steve Chambers, rang me. He had been one of my sub-editors and had left to join ITV where he had done a dangerous stint in Northern Ireland.

'It's Steve Chambers here. You probably don't remember me from the *Daily Telegraph*. You told me I'd never make a sub.'

He added, 'But you taught me more about this business than anybody else.'

He now had a job with the National Council for the Training of Journalists and wondered if I would become a member of his panel, which visited various universities, and centres where journalism was taught? The task was really one of quality control.

Steve was good company and an ideal man for the job, adding much needed experience to what to some extent was a bureaucratic organisation. His reports, which he often gave me to look over, were masterpieces of diplomacy and suggestions. This in turn led me to Brighton where Ian Jones and Paula O'Shea ran one of the best training centres, mostly for postgraduate entrants into journalism. The fact that they were located inside the *Brighton Argus* building and worked closely with the then *Argus* editor was a huge advantage.

I became a fixture on the course, teaching sub-editing and feature writing, despite the 200-mile round trip from Dorset to Sussex. At the same time I continued to visit other centres with and without Steve. Some of the standards were disappointing and occasionally my visits were as welcome as a knock on the door from the Gestapo.

My real criticism lay in the fact that students were given unrealistic hopes about careers in newspapers and magazines. There were far too many chasing too few jobs.

I also taught magazine publishing and management at Solent University one day a week. This organisation could not get into the top 100 universities and I was appalled at some of the staff. There were some shining exceptions, who worked astonishingly well with unsuitable students. But not many.

Some people working in further education feel they deserve more time to spend on research and while this is difficult to fault in many areas the quality and choice of subjects to research, that they select in preference to teaching, is often risible. The priority should always be the students. They also seem to labour under the misapprehension of the dodo: *Everybody has won and all must have prizes.*

As for the students, entry requirements were low, and in any class I would estimate 10% of them were likely to succeed, 30% could perhaps struggle on and the remainder should never have been allowed on the course.

I've never been convinced that it takes three years to qualify as a journalist. One problem is the length of the academic year that occupies only 30 weeks. For many vocational qualifications, such as journalism, why not offer two years with 45 weeks each? It would cut the time needed to qualify and reduce the cost.

Here you run up against the buffers of restrictive practices, the last two bastions of which are no longer the dockers or boilermakers but the academic world and the legal profession. It needs the wealth and vision of billionaires James Dyson of vacuum cleaner fame and Jim Ratcliffe, the entrepreneurial engineer to break the mould. Perhaps Rupert Murdoch could join them. What a trinity that would be! Certainly nobody in Parliament has the vision or the guts.

As I spent more and more time teaching, including switching to creative writing and freelance journalism for adults, I found that older participants were much more likely to progress than 19-year-olds. They were self-selective and easier to teach.

CHAPTER 22

The ball no question makes of ayes or noes but here or there as strikes the player goes

Even allowing for the Santa Maria debacle I have always enjoyed sport. As far as golf goes I have played in Scotland, England, Wales, Ireland and Jersey. In France, Portugal, Spain, Sardinia and Austria. In the United States, the West Indies and Australia. Two shelves of my now much smaller library are filled with golf books. If I could play one more round of my best golf where would it be?

Like most other sports, I tried to make up in enthusiasm what I lacked in skill. Hence I would have to choose Royal Dornoch in Scotland where I shot 76 gross off a handicap of 11 and Walton Heath in Surrey where I scored 41 Stableford points in a heavy drizzle on a Press Golfing Society day to win first prize. There was a stewards' inquiry and demands by fellow journalists for a dope test after that victory as I was four points clear of the field and promptly reduced to an eight handicap in the **PGS!** Thus it proves the point that golfers love courses that love them.

When Rupert Murdoch bought the *News of the World* he found, to his surprise, that the two courses at Walton Heath went with it. As the Digger didn't care for golf he sold it to the members. How Sky TV must have looked back and rued that day.

Royal Dornoch would rival St Andrews which I loved so much I once played it twice in a day with my friend Ted.

We were in Scotland one autumn on a golfing holiday. We played several courses, including Ballater alongside the river Dee and a charming one at Boat of Garten alongside the River Spey. The Boat included a 10-minute wait in a hide to see a pair of Ospreys return to their nest. At Ballater It poured with rain but hot showers and large single malt whiskies prevented pneumonia.

After that we headed for St Andrews, the Holy Grail of golfers.

I had read so much about it that I felt I knew the Old Course. It's time to admit that I have around 150 books on golf. It seems astonishing now but we walked on to the course around noon, paid less than a £1 each, and played the world's most famous course. It was idyllic. No reading had prepared me for the size of the greens that could accommodate a reasonable dance.

On our return to the charming town of St Andrews we were too late for lunch but a kindly waitress suggested high tea, to be followed by some apple tart and cream left over from lunch. If you are about to visit Scotland have a day when you forget about lunch and dinner and have high tea instead.

After the feast Ted wondered what we should do next. Together we decided: let's play it again. And we did, putting out on the 18th in the gloaming. After that experience I suggested to my children that while Oxford, Cambridge and Harvard might be ok, I felt that St Andrews University would be a better target. Sadly none entered that university, favoured by one William Arthur Philip Louis Windsor, the future king of England.

Royal Ashdown in Sussex was another wonderful place to play.

I had my only hole in one at Guadalmina in Spain. In Ireland I loved Killarney and Portmarnock where on the hottest day of the year in 1976 I stripped off completely and went for a cool-down swim in the sea with my host, the managing director of Cochrane and Cantrell, before drying in the sunshine to continue.

In the United States June and I played Mississippi National and watched a mother and three baby alligators cross a fairway 50 yards in front of us. In South Carolina, which has wall-to-wall courses, I played for Britain in a mock Ryder Cup, against the locals. In Sardinia I helped to run golf weeks at Pevero for Rank Hotels with the legendary Dai Rees.

In the West Indies on St Lucia I holed a full-blooded five wood for an eagle. My joy was exceeded by June who hooked a marlin when we went big game fishing. I didn't get a tiddler.

The missed two-foot putts, the shanked drives, the topped five irons I have mostly forgotten. Except...Prestwick. Thanks to *Golfing Magazine* we had a first class four ball lined up there during a visit to the Open at Turnberry. I was playing off 11 and the other three were all single figures. In addition I had a bad cold and felt like death. As all the usual caddies were carrying at the Open, only 'Old Davie' was left and my comrades decided in an unusual spirit of generosity that I could hire him.

Now the first hole at Prestwick, where the Open was born, is one of the most famous opening holes in golf with a brick wall marking out-of-bounds running down the right-hand side from tee to green. On the other side of the wall is a railway. The hole measures only about 345 yards. You need to hit 160 yards to reach the fairway. Around 200 yards will leave a short iron to the green, favour the right side of the fairway for an easier second shot.

As my driver was having one of its many periodic off-spells I asked Davie for a 3 wood. 'Aye, that's all you'll need sir. Anywhere down the middle.'

He clearly thought I was a shrewd player, having noted the keen bargaining that went on over stakes before we teed off. The discussion on amounts for oozlums, sandies, birdies and ferrets had taken up precious time.

I had a practice swish or two and stepped up to the tee. My shot seemed to go straight for about 140 yards and then sliced sharply right heading for the railway. I held my breath as it hit the wall three inches from the top and bounded back into the middle of the fairway.

The other three were a bus ride down the fairway in position A. Caddie Davie was silent. I asked for a five iron, topped it horribly, whereupon it skipped down the middle of the fairway and bounced on to the green about 35 feet from the hole. I think Alliss refers to this, with his gift for oxymorons, as the best bad shot in golf.

The others all lobbed wedges closer to the flag leaving me first to putt. I had bought a new putter at the Open village the previous day and this was its first use in combat. The putt scuttled into the hole for a birdie. Remarks from my fellow players are best left unreported but old Davie had the right phrase for my success. 'D'ya always play as well as this, sir?'

Davie was later matched by a green keeper at Pitlochry. This is a little known but wonderful course overlooking Loch Tummel. On this particular day we had a full spate of Scottish weather from hailstones and a storm to sunshine. On an uphill 400 yarder I had hit a good drive down the middle and reached into the bag for a five wood.

An old green keeper who had been working in a nearby bunker had stepped back politely to let me play the shot. Before I addressed the ball he said, 'It's no a five wood for you.'

Thankful for his advice I asked what he thought I should take. 'A 5 iron.' I hit my 5 iron as sweet as any shot played by Jack Nicklaus. It took off like a plane from an aircraft carrier and soared away. Only to come to a stop some 30 yards short of the green, dead in line with the flag.

I looked at the green keeper. He looked at me. Nobody spoke but I still kept looking at him and refused to walk on. He had resumed raking the bunker but eventually looked up. 'You no hit it properly,' was his verdict.

*   *   *   *

Until golf took over, cricket was my first love. After school and the army I played for Bournemouth Amateurs and Dorchester Casuals. I also covered games at Lord's, the Oval and several other grounds.

Cricket, like golf, seems to attract good writers and commentators. John Arlott was my favourite commentator with Richie Benaud close behind. John used to sit next to me in most Press boxes and I recall a day when we were covering football at West Ham. A few days earlier he had lost a son in an horrific road accident. Nobody really knew what to say but as I was nearest. I put my hand on his shoulder and said, 'we're so sorry to hear this, John.' He nodded his thanks. A few minutes later he passed me his instructions from the *Observer* and said: 'I can't do this John. Can you do it for me?' He left with tears still in his eyes. For fun, as a fellow Hampshire man, I often used to try to imitate his accent. Now I wrote an Arlott report for the *Observer* as well as my own for the *Sunday Express*. Nobody was any the wiser.

At the *Telegraph* Jim Swanton, the magisterial cricket correspondent was treated as reverentially as a bishop. One night an early copy of the *Mail* arrived in the *Telegraph* office saying Brian Close had been sacked as England captain. Nobody else had a line on the story. As Night Editor I asked the Sports Editor, Kingsley Wright, to ring Swanton. Yes, he knew but he was sworn to secrecy and therefore could not and would not write the story.

I spoke to Swanton and we had a brief exchange of views, particularly when I asked him who paid his wages and what was expected from him. I reminded him that it was our duty to publish news, not supress it. He responded that he had never been so insulted in his life and would speak to Lord Hartwell about me the following day. Whatever he said or didn't say, nothing happened.

* * * * *

My one regret as far as racing is concerned is that I have never attended the Grand National. I have backed winners (and many more losers) at Ascot, Goodwood, Cheltenham, Newmarket, Epsom, Sandown, Bath, Salisbury, Wye, Fontwell, Plumpton, Kempton Park, Longchamp, Royal Randwick (Australia) and Sha Tin (Hong Kong).

Longchamp was a memorable occasion. June, Sally, about seven years old, and I went to Paris for a long weekend. We were strolling down the Champs Elysées and while they were spellbound by a mouth-watering show in a magnificent patisserie I was scanning the newsstand outside and chanced upon *Paris Turf,* the equivalent of the now defunct *Sporting Life* racing paper. I bought a copy and was then lured into the patisserie. Reading *Paris Turf* I realised that racing was due to begin at Longchamp in a couple of hours and we caught the metro and then a bus to the course.

There's a wonderful restaurant overlooking the finishing straight and after explaining to the headwaiter that I owned a British racing magazine (I didn't tell him it concerned greyhounds) and this was our first visit to Longchamp we were given a table overlooking the winning post. A 50 franc note helped. To my delight I could easily read the form and noticed several horses from England were among the runners, including some very good ones.

There are no bookmakers allowed in France but there were plenty of windows for the Tote. We ordered a meal and settled down to the more serious business of studying form. By the time I got up to bet (including choices from June and Sally) the cheap windows had long queues and I had to patronise the expensive 100 franc window. This went on all afternoon with attentive staff taking away my meal to keep it warm while I was away. With four good winners it's fair to say that visit paid for our weekend in France. It was sheer luck that I could only get to the expensive Tote window. I've always meant to go back to watch the Arc de Triomphe but so far have not managed it.

With my friend Ted we used to have a weekly Yankee which is 11 bets involving four horses. These comprised six doubles, four trebles and a four-horse accumulator. Total outlay for a £1 stake is £11. Several times we had three out of the four winning which produced an excellent return but never the four.

One memorable coup came from betting on football results. In the early days of fixed odds football coupons you could get 60-1 for forecasting three draws. You didn't need to be a senior wrangler from Cambridge or expert in algorithms to work out that one success a season would show a profit.

Our success came the first week in a December. Fine. The following week we again chose three teams to draw and by a quick perusal of the coupon realised that these were in what the promoters called the short list where the odds were 80-1. For the second week running we collected a chunk of change.

Teams in the short list were those the bookies' experts deemed unlikely to draw.

Hence two weeks before Christmas we were in the money. Off we went to Harrods toy department and the children had new bicycles for Christmas and a Wendy house. Such odds are no longer available.

I've had memorable days out at Ascot, Epsom and Sandown and for people watchers they provide a superb cross section of the human race.

* * * *

On gambling it is pertinent to offer a warning note about casinos. Only the house wins while the only game in which a punter has a chance is Blackjack. Even then you have to be a good card counter and sit in the right hand chair facing the dealer which gives you a little more time for decision making.

Despite visits to casinos in Austria, Portugal, Spain, the USA, France and the UK I have never lost more than £40 or so and occasionally won several hundred pounds. The important thing with winnings is to spend them before you hand them back to the bookmaker or casino. The essential rule? Stop when you are ahead and go home.

The other useful point about casinos is that the food is pretty good and reasonable. They make so much money on the tables that the restaurant doesn't need to show a profit.

One of the biggest bookmakers in London was Corals who had moved into casinos. Joe Coral, who came over from Poland as a refugee from the pogroms in the early part of the last century, was my guest at lunch in the Press Club on a memorable day. We began at the bar and I asked what he would like to drink.

'A scotch please.' A club scotch was duly ordered. At the table: 'any preference on wine Joe?'

'A scotch please' and so it went on. All the time he was lucid, very funny and good company.

I asked if he would like a game of snooker and he was prepared to stay all afternoon. Despite one withered arm he could play a good game, all the time spinning yarn after yarn.

He had started as a street bookmaker in the East End, which was illegal until the Gaming Act of 1961. However, most policemen turned a blind eye to such activities. The only trouble for them was that Joe had a phenomenal memory and didn't need to carry betting slips, as he knew to the penny what he had laid and what he had to pay out. So the local copper used to ask Joe, in a spirit of co-operation, to carry a few betting slips in his pocket so there was sufficient evidence to obtain a conviction for which street bookies were usually fined a fiver. It operated like an unofficial licence.

After our lunch he caught a taxi to the Wig & Pen club, which his son Bernard ran, where he no doubt had another scotch and went home. His company slogan, Never a quarrel bet with Coral, would not have worked with his Polish name: Kagalitsky. His other son, Nick, had inherited his father's flair for business and mathematics.

CHAPTER 23

After June

It's interesting to speculate what and who has had the greatest influence on my life. Tempting, perhaps, to blame setbacks on personality defects or even inherited genes. Being the child of warring parents could be blamed but I feel that surviving such an environment can in fact make you stronger. Should parents who fall out, stay together 'for the sake of the children' or is growing up in a poisonous atmosphere more detrimental? It's the age-old argument of nurture against nature: genes against experiences.

I don't pretend to know the answer but I suspect it's a mixture of both. About the time I went to school my parents had a determined try at saving their marriage. They began to go out regularly together and my uncle Harry used to babysit. This was fine by me because he let me stay up for one game of darts, which often became best of three.

Consequently by the time I went to school my mental arithmetic was red hot. If I needed 55 to win with three darts it was simple: treble 17 with the first dart, then two shots at double two. At the age of eight or nine, when my father was away in the navy I used to go out on bread round with the same uncle. Small loaves were twopence threefarthings and working out the weekly bills involving two small loaves, one large loaf and six rolls was a simple exercise in mental arithmetic to add up pennies, halfpence and farthings.

In another age he should have been a vet and on the family farm in Cornwall, before it was sold, people would often bring a sick horse to him before involving a vet. His main job in Bournemouth was to look after the horses that went out on the bread rounds.

I was also equipped with boxing gloves at the age of four. This meant that occasionally I would get my retaliation in first as all boxers and front row forwards in Wales are advised.

The first man I really admired was my scoutmaster, Captain J H Brough. He had lost both his arms in the First World War but played an active part in the community. He was fiercely independent and many of the boys in his troop went on to great things. He was one of those leaders who effortlessly generate esprit de corps.

We were the 36th Scout Troop and my school troop was the 35th. The six-a-side football tournaments and other contests were keenly fought as several of us Bournemouth schoolboys stayed loyal to the 36th. Often these two troops would figure in the final of the competition. It was a bit like Arsenal and Tottenham: no prisoners were taken.

Bournemouth School had an impressive array of masters but only two made any impact on me. One was Whitman, who looked at my exam results one year and sighed: 'Thank God there's more to life Jenkins than O level chemistry.' He also ran the school cricket team so that probably helped me. My rebellious streak did not prevent him making me house captain. The other was Hickling, who had served as a colonel. He taught English but was equally hot on good manners. Most of the masters had served in WWII and found it easy to keep classes well disciplined. They were more than a match for a bunch of 14-year-old smart Alecs.

One of the shrewdest men was a Physics master called 'Jimmy' James. He and I did not get on and he used to threaten me with a 'season ticket' for Wednesday afternoon detention, which would have wrecked my cricket and football appearances.

Around the age of 14 or 15, after a couple of hours of cricket practice I stopped off in the Five Ways pub for a shandy on the way home. Suddenly, at my elbow, appeared Jimmy James. My heart sank. This was his opportunity to exact full revenge. I would certainly be expelled. But he merely asked me if I was going to have another drink. 'No sir,' I just popped in for one on the way home from cricket.'

He nodded 'good night.'

I lived in fear for around 48 hours but 'Jimmy' did not say a word or even mention it to me again. I never again played up in his class and even got an O level in Physics. What a clever man.

Others whose views I respected were David Francis, the Methodist minister at St George's church in Boscombe, and my Commanding Officer in Vienna, Major Lionel von d'Hardinge. Command came so easily to him, we would have followed him anywhere.

Whether I like to admit it or not my father also had an influence. He took little at face value and showed a substantial degree of cynicism. After not speaking or contacting him for nearly 30 years I decided to trace him. A friend, a former journalist, who worked for the American outfit, Kroll Investigations, found him for me within a few days. I remember the shock when he said: 'I found him, John, but he died a month ago.'

He gave me the address where his widow lived and at Christmas June and I went to visit her in Wells, Somerset. She was a friendly little lady and after initial nervousness gave me a picture of my father with their poodle. She said he had always looked for my name in the *Sunday Express* sports pages when I worked there and got occasional news from one of my aunts. We left her with our best wishes and a Christmas hamper of goodies. She died a couple of years later and we attended her funeral.

CHAPTER 24

Broadcasting nationally and local

I had my first taste of broadcasting with British Forces Network in Austria, enjoyed it and found it interesting. It was very much a seat of the pants operation but I never seriously considered it as a career.

An American colleague at the *Telegraph*, Phil Bangsberg, used to string for the American ABC and on one occasion when I was with him he received a message asking for some vox pop interviews on Eisenhower who had just died. We strolled out into Oxford Street and the first person we approached had served as a liaison officer with Ike's staff in London. New York thought we were amazing.

My exploits with *Retirement Choice* and *Greyhound Magazine* opened several doors and using invitations to appear on various programmes I took the opportunity to publicise my magazines.

Michael Whale did a lunchtime show on LWT and invited me to discuss the Greyhound Derby. This was my first foray into TV and noted with surprise that a chauffeur driven car was sent to collect me, I was greeted warmly, offered coffee or drinks and waited in a plush lounge with TV programmes showing on four different screens.

Michael turned up and off we went to make-up. I thought the run through went pretty well. He asked finally which dog I thought would win?

'Strictly between you and me Michael, and nobody else, Westmead Myra has a great chance.' I thought that was a rehearsal but in fact it went out live and everybody was pleased. A week later I got a cheque which surprised me. My tip? Finished third.

Then I appeared on a Granada programme called Brass Tacks. Also on the show were Jack Jones, the controversial leader of the Transport and General Workers Union, and Maggie Kuhn, leader of an American pensioners group called the Gray Panthers.

The clear aim of the show was to highlight the shortcomings in the British state pension scheme and benefits for pensioners. I have to admit that my two colleagues were better briefed and far more adept at hogging the microphone. Nevertheless it was a good contact.

A few years later Maurice Oldfield, the director of the Allied Lyons Pension Fund, and chairman of the National Association of Pension Funds, wanted a panel to judge the best in-house pension fund newspaper. On that panel he wanted somebody controversial. 'Jack Jones?'

'Splendid,' said Maurice and I arranged for Jones to be one of the judging panel for a modest fee and expenses. We travelled to Bristol by train and that journey was a most interesting two hours. We spent most of the time discussing his experiences fighting against Franco's forces in the Spanish Civil War.

Whether you agree with a man's politics or not you have to respect somebody who feels strongly enough to fight for his beliefs. He was a perfect choice for the role and I ensured I caught the same train back to London with him. Later he was denounced as a spy for Moscow. I had more regard for Jack Jones than I had for Burgess, Philby, Maclean and co.

On radio I hosted a two-hour marathon on Radio Solent, fielding questions about retirement and appeared on a shambles of a programme on LBC. For some reason they thought I was going to talk about gardening. Nobody could be more ill suited to that task than me. I ad-libbed on the state of the Press.

Nowadays I broadcast twice a week on a local station on current affairs. It really just fills in a gap between music programmes and a few bits of local news.

Would I have enjoyed working full time in broadcasting? I think I was more suited to the written word.

However, I have nothing but admiration for Tom Mangold, Keith Graves, Harry Weisbloom and John

Humphrys who transferred from newspapers to broadcasting.

As for what appears as fake news or even on social media reports, I despair at the lack of discipline and editorial control. Many of these outlets glory in power without responsibility, a charge once falsely laid at the door of journalism by Stanley Baldwin. They transcend national boundaries and appear accountable to nobody. Another weasel moment which really irks me is a BBC news item which begins: 'The BBC has learned that...' which goes on to quote a story which the Beeb read in the previous day's *Mirror* or *Times*.

Nevertheless social media is more responsible for the huge decline in newspaper and magazine sales than broadcasters.

As an adjunct to journalism, in recent years I have lectured at writing festivals as diverse as Santa Barbara in California, Geneva, Cheltenham, Winchester, Durham and Caerleon.

This led naturally to a series of classes on creative writing and freelance journalism. As a further spin off I have edited several books for people. Two were great successes: the *Wines of Chablis* by Owen Smith, a golfing friend from Brockenhurst and *D'Arcy and Elizabeth*, a sequel to Jane Austen's *Pride and Prejudice* written by Frances Morgan.

The first came about when Owen, a considerable wine buff, opened the conversation one Sunday morning by asking me: 'You know something about this publishing racket John, don't you?'

He and a friend had been commissioned to write the book on Chablis by Cassells who had had a shake up in management then changed their minds despite paying him an advance. The manuscript had been delivered in good time and revised by the authors.

We negotiated the release of all rights to the book and the upshot was that Owen, having done the work, wanted to self-publish the book as a hardback, with a full colour jacket and a print order of 3,000 copies. I pointed out the risks and how difficult it was to sell such a book. I also pointed out that £19.99 was a lot to ask. He pointed out the opportunities and that £19.99 was not a lot compared to a good bottle of wine.

So we went ahead. Within a couple of years he was proved right and sold the lot to great acclaim...and substantial profit.

Frances described herself as a retired cook and was so quiet and modest it was hard to believe the ambition to write burned in her soul. Her sequel to *Pride and Prejudice* was not just a simple act of parody or even hero worship. It was a story that re-entered the minds and manners of the couple and projected the hurdles that such a union between an aristocrat and middle class virgin could confront.   I was disappointed that after editing the book I could not interest a publisher or an agent to take it on. We collected many admiring replies but no contract.

We turned to self-publishing. As I have told all my clients, I cannot guarantee to make you any money but I will certainly save you a great deal. Sometimes the costs charged by 'self publishing' companies are so inflated that they are really nothing more than vanity publishers: particularly when it comes to printing, marketing and selling the book.

To limit Frances Morgan's expenditure I advised that she should begin with an order of 300 copies and utilise print on demand. I gave her a modest marketing plan and she took to it like the manor born. Before long she was speaking every week at women's lunches, appearing on radio and television and covering the country from Hay on Wye to Bath. At the latter venues she and her companion, dressed in the clothes of Jane Austen's day, sold copies from a Hansom Cab, if not like hot cakes, certainly like warm buns. Soon she was ordering 1,000 copies a time.

Two other books which I enjoyed editing were: *The Odyssey of Lieut George Trinick,* who served aboard the battle cruiser HMS Temeraire in the First World War and *When the Clouds Roll By,* by Jennie Sherborne, a family history which included the life and times of her father, Spitfire Test pilot George Pickering.

Jennie went on to write a first-class novel, *Give Us this Day,* based on research she did for her family history.

Through editing Jennie's books I came across Lady Houston who had financed the development of the Spitfire. I set to and wrote the first draft of her biography that was short listed for the Biographers' Club main award and will hopefully appear this year after a third re-write. You can read the synopsis at the end of this book.

As publisher of *Writers' Forum* I was in demand at literary festivals, giving talks on various aspects of writing – from freelance journalism to self-publishing, editing to marketing.

The friendliest festival was Caerleon in Wales where people returned year after year. The best organised was at Cheltenham where an efficient staff had everything organised down to the last comma, and the best in every respect was in Santa Barbara, California, the brainchild of Barnaby Conrad.

Barney started with a huge advantage in terms of location: 100 miles north of Los Angeles and some 400 miles south of San Francisco where he had owned a nightclub after writing *Matador*, a best seller that sold more than three million copies. He had a galaxy of writers on call from Hollywood and the Pacific coastal resorts.

Barney was a true polymath in the Hemingway mould. After the University of North Carolina, where he was captain of boxing, he studied painting at the University of Mexico, where he also became interested in bullfighting. After being injured in the bullring, he returned to college and graduated from Yale in 1943. He wanted to join the Navy but his bullfighting injury prevented that. He was American Vice Consul in Seville, Málaga, and Barcelona from 1943-46. While in Spain, he studied bullfighting with Belmonte and Manolete, later appearing on the same programme with Belmonte when he was awarded the ears of the bull.

In 1947 he worked as secretary to novelist Sinclair Lewis, the first American writer to win the Nobel Prize for literature.

Barney published his first novel, *The Innocent Villa*, in 1948. It went unnoticed, but his second novel, *Matador*, hit the jackpot. He went on to write more than 30 books, many on the craft of writing.

Boxing, bullfighting, nightclubs, writing and the navy. It would have been strange had we not become friends.

The workshops and speakers at Santa Barbara were excellent and delegates put in sometimes 10 and 12 hours work each day to polish their style. Workshop leaders were expected to know their stuff and the whole atmosphere was inspiring, educational and fun.

The problem with many British festivals is that some authors turn up just to plug their own books when many of the audience wish to learn something about writing. Sometimes the main aim often seems just to make money for the promoters.

I went to a festival in Harrogate devoted to crime writing where Colin Dexter of Morse fame, talked amusingly about his life as a writer and his character Morse.

At Winchester and other venues he made exactly the same speech and signed just as many books.

Deadlines all my Life

CHAPTER 25

Skeletons and honours

I opened this record by following my advice to other would-be biographers – begin at the turning point in your life. My second piece of advice is that you cannot go back in a family history more than two generations before skeletons begin to fall out of the cupboard. That makes your story even more interesting.

Baddies make better stories than goodies.

My own family is no exception. My mother's family are as Cornish as saffron cake, cream and pasties and my father's as South London as the Old Kent Road, Manor Place Baths, East Street Market and the Elephant and Castle.

I was born in the more genteel watering hole of Bournemouth but have still shared many of the influences – for good and ill – from Cornwall and the Old Kent Road.

My father's family, originated in Wales but like many people from the valleys who bred and trained pit ponies, emigrated to London in the 19th century where they thought the streets were paved with gold. Most of them became milkmen, cabbies or bread deliverymen for horses were the main form of transport.

My grandfather had four hansom cabs on the road, one of which he drove himself and the other three were piloted by hired drivers. They navigated around London not by the A – Z street booklet or satnav but by pubs.

To get from Walworth Road to St Paul's he would give his drivers directions via various pubs en route, The George, the Thomas A Becket, the Elephant and Castle, the Hoop and Grapes and so on.

Perhaps his most famous watering hole was the Thomas A Becket, an ornate late-Victorian landmark no longer echoing to the thud of leather on the heavy bag or skipping in the upstairs gym and the noisy snuffle that boxers make in training. It was mentioned in the Canterbury Tales as the first stop which pilgrims made on the way to the Thomas A Becket shrine in Canterbury but during the 20th century was the epicentre of the local boxing scene with an upstairs gym where our heavyweight champion Henry Cooper trained with his brother Jim under the beady eye of their manager Jim Wicks.

There have been several attempts to revive it as a trendy watering hole that would have outraged my grandfather.

My favourite, on his list for many years, was the George in Southwark, the last galleried inn in London. There was a time when Shakespeare's plays were performed on low loaders parked together to make a stage in the courtyard.

That too has now joined the trendy list. There has been a pub on this site since the 16th century and in 1677 the George was rebuilt after a serious fire that destroyed most of medieval Southwark. Dickens liked it and mentioned it in *Little Dorrit*.

When teaching Howard to drive I would make him go to London from East Grinstead. We would drive past Kennington Oval, across Westminster Bridge, along Whitehall, around Trafalgar Square down Fleet Street and across the river to Southwark where we stopped at the George for a much-needed half pint to steady our nerves.

Dr Mervyn Stockwood, the Bishop of Southwark, was often there. He dabbled in spiritualism, and derived assurance for his episcopal policies from paranormal sources, not always to the approval of his fellow churchmen. He was also said to be a favourite of Princess Margaret, rushing to her defence when her lifestyle was criticised. He would stand modestly at the bar with a half of real ale, an excellent brew from Norfolk.

Like any episcopal eccentric Stockwood was a gift to Fleet Street. He believed that a broken ankle he suffered was healed when a woman who 'possessed remarkable healing powers' laid her hands upon it. He was so convinced that he asked the woman to heal his cat, Midge, who was arthritic.

My grandfather certainly knew the George and while his horse would have a drink at the trough he would enjoy a quick pint. By the time he got to Hampstead he would have consumed several pints.

One Christmas present from my uncles in London was a pair of roller skates so I got to know the Walworth Road area pretty well. In Manor Place my grandfather had once kept his horses and cabs. My father used to regale me with stories how he had to get up at 5a.m. break the ice in the trough in the yard to wash and take a couple of horses to the farriers to be shod before he went to school. Those stables had become a workshop and garage for two of my uncles who were car nuts. I remember a Lagonda and an Alvis beautifully restored.

The local baths survived heavy bombing in the blitz. My grandparents were not so lucky and were, in the phrase of the day, bombed out. For a while they stayed with us in Bournemouth. Strange that I should return to Manor Place Baths to cover boxing for the *Evening Standard*. The baths closed as a public facility in 1976 but continued as a boxing venue until a final show in 1978. The Krays were among many who had fought there.

Despite moving to Bournemouth my grandparents did not escape the bombing but arrived in time for a daylight raid by 26 Focke Wolf 190s. Nearly 200 people, mostly Allied airmen staying at the Metropole Hotel, died in the Luftwaffe raid on 23 May 1943. The aircraft dropped 25 high-explosive bombs on the town, destroying 22 buildings and damaging a further 3,000. They also machine-gunned the town as they swept over at rooftop height. One cannon shell ripped through a door eight inches above my head. I was sitting on the doorstep. After my parents divorced I lost touch with my father's family.

My mother's family in Cornwall had no easy life. Cornwall, a hotbed of the Liberal Party and Methodist chapels, relied on three main ways to earn a living: mining, fishing or farming. None of them paid that well. The family did however, include in its family tree an innkeeper or two, a blacksmith, a worker in serpentine, and sundry other trades. No doubt they also took part and enjoyed the benefits of smuggling through Coverack and looting the wrecks that piled up on the rocks in the 18th and 19th centuries. It is also claimed that we have a bigamist in the family.

How my grandfather worked his way up from farm labourer to tenant farmer on the Lizard I have never been told. He had, however, a good basic education for those times, unlike my grandmother who signed her wedding certificate with an x.

It was a struggle for all his life with the farm saved first by the desperate need for horses in World War I and the need to cultivate every square inch in World War II. Between the wars it was little more than subsistence farming. They survived on the milk cheque and eggs, butter and chickens my grandmother took to market plus the occasional bed and breakfast visitor.

The family also took part in the greatest sea rescue carried out by one of Britain's most successful and best-run charities: The Royal National Lifeboat Institution. It is tempting to use George Schultz's cartoon character Snoopy's beginning for this remarkable story: *It was a dark and stormy night.*

But then, most times that RNLI craft put to sea in an emergency it is a dark and stormy night. Liners and cargo ships do not run aground or hit rocks in daylight in calm waters.

On that dark and stormy night of March 17th/18th 1907 the White Star liner Suevic ran on to rocks off the Cornish coast.

To rescue more than 400 souls, including women and 70 babies in rough seas was a triumph for the four Cornish lifeboats stationed on the Lizard, and at the fishing villages of Porthleven, Cadgwith and Coverack.

The totals were shared by Cadgwith 227, Coverack 44, the Lizard boat 167 and Porthleven 18. The remainder were saved by tugs sent to rescue the Suevic.

The boats were crewed by local volunteers: fishermen who knew the seas as well as their own country lanes, yeoman farmers, labourers and even a clerk in holy orders.

Neither Drake nor Bluebeard could have wished for a more dedicated and muscular crew. And muscular they had to be for the little wooden craft depended on six men, each with an oar. These craft were all open-topped rowing boats fewer than 40 feet in length.

The boat from the Lizard was named after Admiral Sir George Beck (35 feet) the Melanie Moon from Cadgwith (39 feet) the Constance Melanie from Coverack (35 feet) and the John Frances White from Porthleven which was the smallest at 32 feet. All were designed to be self-righting in the event of capsizing and carried the names of those who had contributed wholly or partly to their cost.

First on the scene were the boats from the Lizard and Cadgwith just in time to prevent a disaster as two lifeboats from the liner were in danger of being dashed to pieces on hidden rocks.

Ashore, the wives and daughters of the lifeboat crews waded into the surf to collect the infants from their mothers' arms and keep them safe from the pounding surf. Every tiny cottage was thrown open and warm drinks, blankets and food provided for the shipwrecked passengers.

As each lifeboat unloaded its precious crew, it put about to return to the stricken Suevic. The rescue went on for 16 hours of back-breaking toil, danger and quiet heroism. As the regular oarsmen were overcome with fatigue a relay of volunteers stepped forward to take their place. My grandfather and many others took their turn at the oars.

Last to leave were the crew of the Suevic who had played their part in the rescue. According to the official RNLI report:

The drama began shortly after 10.30pm during a vicious storm with thick fog covering the Lizard peninsular. The gloom was briefly pierced by the red glow of a distress rocket. The flare, accompanied by the eerie sound of a ship's horn rising above the howling gale, was recognised by villagers in the fishing communities near the notorious, treacherous rocky outcrop.

The passengers and crew aboard the stricken SS Suevic did not yet know it but the largest - and perhaps the greatest rescue in the history of the RNLI - had begun. Every person was saved – even a stowaway and the ship's cat.

The 12,000-ton Suevic, owned by the White Star Line which two years later commissioned the SS Titanic, was on the final leg of a voyage from Australia to England on 17 March 1907 when it hit the Menheere Reef - a belt of half-submerged rocks off the Lizard.

The rescue was accomplished with remarkable bravery and sang froid, from the village women who waded into the waves in darkness to carry children the last few yards to shore, to the captain of the Suevic who conducted the evacuation while smoking his cigar, and to the Cornish vicar who led the rescue from one of the boats.

All that the lifeboat crews, who made their living fishing for pilchard and mackerel, had to protect themselves from the elements were their oilskins and basic cork life belts. Such was the fog on the night of the rescue and the difficulties caused by a strong south-westerly, the crew of the first lifeboat to get to the Suevic only knew they had reached their destination when they smashed into liner's hull, throwing one of them overboard. Fortunately the crew pulled him back on board. Peter Greenslade, secretary of the Lizard lifeboat, said: 'We know that at times the rowers were barely stemming the tide as they pulled against the prevailing conditions. They were in open boats and at the mercy of the sea. It must have been terrifying and yet they went back to the Suevic time and time again. The rescue operation involved the lifeboats rowing up to four miles out to the liner, which was stuck fast on the rocks. They had to take on board survivors as the waves lifted them level with the decks of the liner. Those on board the Suevic included 85 children, of whom 60 were younger than three. The passengers were ferried to the nearby coves, where women from the villages had lit fires to guide the lifeboats and warm the survivors.'

The official RNLI history of the incident recorded how two crewmen on the Suevic distinguished themselves in the perilous procedure to load the infants into the waiting lifeboats.

"They carried the children down the rope ladders and when the lifeboats, which were surging up and down, rose on the waves, dropped them into the arms of the lifeboatmen, who tended them until the mothers were lowered over the side and, steadied by the men, were also skilfully dropped into the boats."

One of the two sailors, George Anderson, said afterwards: 'It was a trying task but, lord, to see those mothers clasp their bairns to their breasts and to hear their thanks and God bless you made me feel that I could have swum ashore with all the babies in the ship.'

Prominent among the rescuers was the Reverend Henry Vyvyan, a vicar in Cadgwith and secretary of the village's lifeboat - an honorary position that did not normally involve putting out to sea.

On this occasion, the vicar was determined to take part. He jumped from the Cadgwith lifeboat to one of the two ships' boats and safely guided it back to land. When he tried to return to the Suevic with that boat, the sailors were unable to cope and it was smashed on the rocks. Unperturbed, Vyvyan swam back to shore and waited for the Lizard lifeboat to return, whereby he 'proceeded to the wreck where he assisted generally and superintended taking the passengers on board.' Describing how he steered the Suevic lifeboat to shore, he said: 'I went on board to steer her but soon found the six men could hardly pull against the wind. I can tell you I felt jolly proud when she touched the beach and all the women and children were landed safely. Directly I landed my passengers, I stood up in the bows of the boat and called for volunteers to go back with me.' His call was quickly answered.

The rescue continued through the night, with no let-up between 3am and 4am when the weather was foulest, until the last passenger was brought to safety at midday the next day. Together, the four lifeboats saved 456 people. The remaining 68 passengers and crew were taken on board by three tugs sent by White Star to salvage its stranded liner. With typical understatement, the RNLI history stated: 'The indomitable pluck and perseverance displayed by all during the service was much appreciated.'

Six rescuers, including Vyvyan and the two crewmen from the Suevic, were given the RNLI's silver medal - its second highest award for gallantry. What, I wonder, do people have to do to get the top award?

Bob Drew, 58, a retired police officer whose family came from Cadgwith, had three relatives in the crew of the village's lifeboat that night. His great-great-uncle, Edwin Rutter, was the coxswain of the vessel and one of those to receive the silver medal. Mr Drew said: 'I think they were incredibly brave to head off in that thick fog and darkness when they knew the dangers they would face.'

The empty liner suffered an unusual fate. Reluctant to write off its vessel, White Star Line commissioned salvagers to sever the bow of the liner stuck on the rocks by blowing it up with dynamite. The remainder of the ship, which was still afloat, was then towed to Southampton, where it was fitted with a new bow made by Harland & Wolff, the Belfast shipyard. Renamed Skytteren, the Suevic was eventually scuttled by its crew in1940 off the Swedish coast to prevent its capture by the Nazis.

The modern conception of ocean liners is one of unparalleled luxury but the Suevic and her sister ships had large accommodation for steerage passengers – the cheapest form of travel. Survivors from the Suevic were not celebrities draped in fur and diamonds (like the Titanic) but many travelling steerage class. Supper was not five courses with wine in a sumptuous dining room.

One passenger reported: *It was St Patrick's Day and most people on the Suevic homeward bound from Australia were wearing green rosettes. We were due to dock in Plymouth where the first-class passengers would leave us and we would go on to Southampton.*

At about eight o' clock we had our usual supper of bread and cheese, sometimes it was biscuits and cake. We supplemented this with our own supplies of cocoa and potted ham. (I sometimes wonder what modern passengers would say to such a supper but then, they would pay more than £24 for their passage).

Outside the fog had closed in shrouding everything and the foghorn sounded drearily. Sleep seemed the most attractive prospect.

It was almost 10.30 as I took my coat off before lying down when I was suddenly thrown to one side.

There was a tremendous crash. The vessel heaved up and lurched forward. For a time it shivered and shook, then stopped – and silence. It was a strange sort of silence as though everyone on the ship was motionless. Suddenly the corridors began to fill as people raced out asking questions nobody could answer.

On deck the ship seemed steady but at a slight angle. The captain passed us by saying 'Keep calm; we are only grounded. Nothing to worry about. Trust me. Tell other people not to panic and come up on deck with warm clothing.'

Our group decided to stay together as we were instructed to go on deck.

All lowering of boats had stopped and the last one hung stuck halfway down the ship's side. They waited there miserable and cold before being rescued five hours later.

As the lifeboats from the shore came alongside passengers had to climb down a rope ladder and judge when it was safe to let go as the lifeboat rose and fell alarmingly in the swell. Hour after hour we waited our turn.

At 10 o clock my turn came. As the boat rose on a wave an officer yelled let go and I found myself in the arms of three sailors who settled me in a place and made me comfortable. Once in the boat I actually slept until the boat bumped on the beach. We were in Cadgwith four miles from the Lizard. One friendly woman took five of us to her cottage for a wonderful breakfast.

Sixty years later Hilda Tresidder, who wrote this account, revisited Cadgwith and talked to a fisherman who had been in the lifeboat that had rescued so many people. Coverack, once notorious for smugglers and wreckers, had polished its reputation.

* * * *

As soon as she was able my mother parked me on my grandparents in Cornwall for 18 months as she and my father were both working. Pictures and family stories have told me of the idyllic existence in which I was totally spoiled by my grandparents, aunts and uncles. In fact my grandmother cried when I left the farm. You would have thought she would have had enough of children, having had 15 who survived.

Perhaps it was no surprise that my son has become an American citizen as four of my mother's family sought their fortune in the new world. Little was heard from them apart from one of my uncles who came back to the UK for a visit on his retirement. He had spent a while trapping furs for the Hudson Bay company, taken a job with Anaconda Copper and then set up a business repairing car radiators.

One hidden scandal concerned a mother who ran off with her daughter's husband but that was never spoken about in front of the children. My mother, like most of her generation, believed that family scandals were best kept hidden.

She was more forthcoming about her service in World War I. She enlisted in the Women's Army Auxiliary Corps and was posted to Sandhurst where she was a waitress. Desperate for men at the front, all the stewards had been posted to France. The passing out parade with the adjutant riding his horse down the steps of the Royal Military College left a lasting impression on her.

A few years ago I found that Trevenwith's most important crop were caravans but lately it has become a centre for Friends of the Earth.

The story of the RNLI rescue, and the fact that my son is a master mariner, is one of the reasons why £2 from the sale of each copy of this book will be divided between the RNLI and Macmillan Cancer Research that was so supportive during the last days of my dear wife. They were swift to act, efficient and compassionate.

I hope you enjoyed my story.

Deadlines all my Life

Index

My next book will be a biography of the lady who saved the Spitfire

Lady Spitfire

Poppy Radmall tip-tapped across the stage in the pantomime chorus at Drury Lane wondering whether to accept an invitation to supper with a young man waiting at the stage door with a bouquet of gardenias.

Such men were mashers in the Cockney slang of the chorus girls who were ambushed nightly as they left the theatre. For some it was just supper and a dance at the Café Royal. To others it might mean something more: rewarded with a diamond clip or a gold bracelet. Such was life in London in the 1870s.

For Poppy, that night spelt the end of innocence and the beginning of a full-on love affair. For her masher, twice her age, debonair and wealthy, it was also love. But Freddie Gretton, heir to the Bass brewing millions, was already married.

To cement their love the couple fled to Paris where they lived as man and wife in the heady days at the end of the 19th century. From the mistresses of other wealthy men and the style of *les grandes horizontales* Poppy rocketed from her lowly origins to join a world in which the Prince of Wales with Lilly Langtry were the leaders of a fashionable, louche society. She learned how to behave in society and how to misbehave with discretion.

This is the saga of how a petite, 16-year-old chorus girl with a beguiling smile and bewitching figure joined society, shocked society, rocked the political establishment and played a huge role in saving Britain.

Three marriages, a divorce and countless lovers after Gretton had died, Poppy Radmall, became Lady Brinckman, then Lady Byron and finally Lady Houston, the richest widow in England with a yacht to match her status. She was also a suffragette, a philanthropist who supported great causes and a pamphleteer to scorch Prime Ministers and appeasers of Hitler and followers of Stalin.

She knew and courted everybody. From Prime Ministers Stanley Baldwin and Ramsay MacDonald to Kipling and Edward VIII, from press Lords Beaverbrook and Rothermere to editors and adventurers. Churchill was her unrequited love and air ace Lord Sempill one of her heroes.

Men of action she admired. Procrastinators and prevaricators she despised. She became a racehorse owner, magazine proprietor and maverick political entrepreneur.

Many men had loved her. Many men had proposed to her – including the poet Walter Savage Landor who was distraught at her rejection – but this wise-in-the-ways of-the-world, merry widow needed nobody after Gretton had left her £7000 a year for life in his will and Lord Houston £6million and a stupendous yacht.

She was the sixth woman to be a Dame of the British Empire, an honour she took seriously.

In 1931, with Ramsay MacDonald as Britain's first Labour Prime Minister, Vickers needed £100,000 government support to win the Schneider Trophy air race outright for the third time and lay the foundation for a new fighter. MacDonald refused. Colonel Sempill, a famous aviator and World WR 1 hero, (later a spy for Japan) went to Lady Houston and explained the position. Could she help?

Yes. She had her cheque for £100,000 (about £6million in today's money) delivered to the Royal Aero Club. The result was the Vickers Supermarine seaplane – designed by R J Mitchell and powered by Rolls Royce - which took the trophy and later set a new airspeed record at 407mph.

It was the forerunner of Mitchell's Spitfire and without Lady Houston's support the Spit would have been too late for the Battle of Britain.

She financed the first flight over Everest and offered the government £200,000 in 1931 to protect London from air attack. The gift was refused. More than 20,000 civilians died in the Luftwaffe blitz on London.

Government inertia and appeasement galvanised her into political action. She bought the ailing *Saturday Review* and used it to berate Baldwin and MacDonald.

The circulation soared.

She decorated her yacht with huge banners attacking the Prime Minister. She sailed it to fleet reviews and around the coast advertising his shortcomings. She also made life a misery for his supporters fighting by-elections by financing their opponents.

She was a strong supporter of Edward VIII and dismayed when he was forced to abdicate. She appealed to the Queen that he should stay.

Lady Houston died in December 1936 a short while before her warnings of another war became true. To the RAF pilots who dipped their wings in salute every time they passed over her yacht or her house she had one final title:

Lady Spitfire.

It's my privilege to tell her story.

An ideal gift offer

If you enjoyed this book and have a friend who would also like the story why not make it a gift? You can order direct from the author for the special price of £8.99 which includes postage and packing and £2 which will go to Macmillan Cancer and the RNLI charities. Your order will be processed within 10 days.

Many thanks,
John Jenkins

Please send me an additional copy of Deadlines All My Life for which I enclose my cheque for £8.99.

Complete in block capitals please.

Name...

Address...

....

Post code...

Post your order to: John Jenkins, 10 Meadow Court, Newtown Lane, Verwood, BH31 6LY.